Classroom
of
Choice

Classroom of Choice

A Teacher's Guide to Creating a Dynamic Classroom

Barbara Szatañski

·

Cecilia Taaffe

Cebra Publishing
Ottawa   Canada

Copyright © 1999 by Cebra Publishing

Canadian Cataloguing in Publication Data

Szatañski, Barbara, 1958-
    Classroom of Choice: a teacher's guide to creating a dynamic classroom

Includes bibliographical references.
ISBN 0-9684173-0-2

  1. Teaching.   I. Taaffe, Cecilia, 1952-   II. Title.

LB1025.3.S93 1998   371.102   C98-900906-8

Front cover photo: © Michael T. Carlon 1998
Text Design by Christine Buechler
Cover Design by Peter Buechler
Author photographs © Michael T. Carlon 1998
Clip art: Nova Development - Art Explosion

Permission to reprint CCDS granted by Dr. Sharon Lapkin, Modern Language
Centre, OISE, 252 Bloor St . West, Toronto, ON M5S 1V6.

Printed in Canada by
Dollco Printing
2340 St. Laurent Blvd.
Ottawa
K1G 6E3

Published by
Cebra Publishing
P.O.Box 41063
Elmvale R.P.O.
1910 St. Laurent Blvd.
Ottawa, Ontario
K1G 5K9

Here's what educators are saying about
Classroom of Choice

"This is a stimulating irresistible guidebook that provides in detail the practical "know-how" to implement current educational theory. Novice and experienced educators will find their passion for teaching enkindled. As an administrator it is difficult to resist the temptation to return to the classroom. The thought of actually applying the strategies shared in this book is enthralling."

Joanne Monahan,Principal
Phi Delta Kappa President,
University of Ottawa Chapter

*"**Classroom of Choice** is an excellent reference and resource that would be of tremendous benefit to any teacher. For those teachers new to learning centres, this book offers an abundance of 'hows' and 'whys' for making the process painless. For others who are already comfortable with child-centred learning, it provides a multitude of new ideas for centres. The more than 100 blackline masters are extremely useful and will expand and enrich their current programmes. In addition, the book offers helpful suggestions for effective timetabling and for the organization and maintenance of consistent assessment records of student achievement."*

Cheryl Tweedy-Hoganson,
4th year Teacher
Smiths Fall, Ontario

"We have all read the theory of how to change our teaching practices. This book gives us the opportunity to put into practice the theory. Barbara and Cecilia have given us a blueprint, a runway to soar! For me, this is exactly what I needed to have - a reference for all the theory rolled into the actual classroom."

Mary Ann Norman,
Teacher/Learning Disabilities Specialist
Roanoke, Virginia, U.S.A.

*"As a new teacher starting out, you are often looking for resources that provide you with guidance and innovative ideas. **Classroom of Choice** is a book that will help in developing your own classroom and teaching style. It provides a framework that you can take into any elementary school classroom, at any grade level, and develop your own dynamic classroom. The book is straight forward, easy to read, and practical to follow. **Classroom of Choice** is a book that I would definitely recommend!"*

Christine Richardson,
First year Teacher
Ottawa, Ontario

Dedicated to the ones I love,
Kevin, my friend, my companion.
Kristopher and Geoffrey, my heart and soul.
And in loving memory of my father, and to my mother, who always taught me
that if you persevere, you can do anything.
B.Sz.

To my husband, Greg,
who has been unfailing in his support of me throughout this project.
To our daughters, Natalie, Erin, and Laura
who have put up with my many absences and hours of work.
To my mother, Laura, who always challenged me to pursue dreams,
and in loving memory of my father
who was one of my first great teachers.
C.T.

ACKNOWLEDGMENTS

Nothing happens until first a dream.
— *Carl Sandburg*

There are many people who contributed to making this dream a reality.

We would like to give our sincere thanks to all those teachers who applauded our work and who in their pleading, "Put it in a book, please?" gave us the courage to take the plunge and produce this book.

We couldn't have developed such a wealth of material and expertise in empowering children with their own learning without the real "movers and shakers" - the many students who have passed through our doors (and in some cases stayed for up to fours years!). In their time with us, they have contributed many valuable insights, tested and helped us refine countless resources, and reflected with us on the effects to their learning. A big thank you and we'd love to hear from you as you develop through your life. Their parents have been a great source of support both in and out of the classroom.

We feel privileged to have had such talented and competent editors, Dr. Nancy Halsall, Carson Stratton, and Martha Milne, who all have played a role beyond refining our text, as friend, mentor, colleague, teacher, and advocate. Thank you to Nancy, too, for encouraging us to practise the craft of writing and proving to ourselves that this was indeed a do-able project.

Thank you to the people of the Carleton Board of Education who have supported our endeavours. Special appreciation and thanks to principals with whom we have worked: Leslie Hossack, John Davidson, Nancy Gobel, and Sandra Richardson; to superintendents John Beatty and Michael Carlon; and to our many colleagues over the years with whom we've had the pleasure of working. Special thanks to Nathaly Roy, a French immersion teacher who translated and had the courage to pilot our model in her early French immersion primary classes.

Thank you to our student teachers from the University of Ottawa, University of Maine, and Queen's University who have practised with us and for allowing us to practise with them.

For legal and financial advice, we feel privileged to have been able to turn to the expertise of Margo Korneluk, Cynthia Sams, Marion Bailey, and Pamela Greene.

To get the crowning bit of advice we needed, we turned to Looneyspoons™ author and publisher, Janet Podleski. She generously gave us her time and personal experience with the publishing world. We are eternally grateful for her parting words, "You would be crazy not to do this!"

Without the patience, artistry, expertise, and devotion of both Christine and Peter Buechler, we could not have the end result as polished looking as it is. And yes, Peter, we will give your company as many plugs as we can! Visit their web site at: www.golden.net/~pmagic.

We wish to thank members of the Phi Delta Kappa University of Ottawa Chapter for first acknowledging our work in their Awards of Excellence program which thereby gave us the confidence to believe in ourselves and share our material with a larger audience. And further for allowing us to practise our publishing/writing/editing skills as co-editors of PDK News/ Nouvelles.

With gratitude to Mary Ann Norman for suggesting just the right title for our book. Her continued correspondence and collegial rapport over the years have been greatly enjoyed.

Ron Benson's wit, expertise, and generosity have delighted us and taught us that the busiest people can give so freely.

To the seven Taaffe siblings who have listened and advised us on educational and commercial interests, a sincere thanks.

And finally, we have to give thanks to our families, who had to endure the endless hours of us talking about this project, being on the computer (until we became part of the furniture) or vying for the use of the telephone. The quote of the hour had to be "Get off the phone!!" which was used with equal frequency by all parties. But all in all, they gave us great support throughout this project.

FOREWORD

As a teacher, principal, co-ordinator, instructor, and course director, Ron Benson's experience in education spans more than thirty years. He is currently practicum supervisor in the teacher education programme at York University, Toronto. He is co-author of Collections published by Prentice Hall Ginn; author of The Writing Handbook published by Ginn Canada; and author of Beginnings... teaching and learning in the kindergarten published by Irwin.

In these days of great challenge in the teaching profession, it's refreshing to read about optimism in the classroom. And **Classroom of Choice** is just that . . . a hopeful, kaleidoscopic look at programming for children in elementary classrooms.

The authors are practising classroom teachers whose commitment to the children, to themselves, and to each other is obvious. They learn from the children, they learn from professional development, and they learn from one another. They exemplify those teachers who, as lifelong learners themselves, are dedicated to the transfer of their love of learning to the children they teach.

The programme they describe is learning centre-based and the classroom areas they detail are extensive— ranging from the more expected (art and painting, books, puzzles, mathematics, sand . . .), through those frequently found in centre-based classrooms (research, science, construction . . .) to some new centre possibilities (video, story study, technology tools, recording . . .). Accompanying the identification of the myriad centres is a comprehensive description of each that includes its purpose, a "what you will need" listing, and a comment from the authors to explain how the centre works. This section of the book will be well-received by those teachers who are embarking on a more learning centre-based approach to programming, and by those who are constantly searching for new ideas to infuse into the learning environments they design with the children.

This approach to implementing and augmenting prescribed curriculum requires that teachers be able to organize numbers of children; involve them in a variety of learning opportunities; and manage the environment as the children engage in reading, writing, calculating, estimating, experimenting, researching, painting, dramatizing . . . ! To provide assistance, the authors have included a compendium of practical suggestions for arranging the classroom and managing the environment in ways that are effective, satisfying, and efficient for both the teacher and the children.

The authors focus attention on evaluation and authentic assessment by discussing the current perspective on this timely and important topic and by furnishing teachers with a variety of assessment strategies necessary to ensure that a comprehensive learning profile results for each child.

Following an extensive professional bibliography is an expansive section of blackline masters and classroom overheads that are cross-referenced to the relevant chapters in the text. Teachers will find these inclusions beneficial in reducing their preparatory workloads so their time can be spent readying the environment in preparation for the implementation of a complementary programme.

The premise of this book is that teachers DO have choice and that they are constantly selecting from a variety of alternatives as they move through their teaching day. It is the authors' belief that children have the right to make learning choices as well. And so, they contend that the classroom should be one in which both teachers and children engage in making important decisions cooperatively and collaboratively.

The vitality of the classroom the authors describe is easily imagined throughout this text and their dynamism and synergy flow from their words. Through their vivid descriptions, they make this reader want to spend time in their classroom to learn alongside them and the children - teachers and children working together to acquire knowledge, to practise skills, and to enjoy the many facets of the learning process. Their classroom is certainly one in which partnerships exist and a community of learners emerges.

I expect that practising teachers who read **Classroom of Choice** will find unlimited practical suggestions they will be able to implement immediately in their classrooms. As well, I foresee that those student teachers who spend time with this text will be treated to innumerable ideas they will be able to practise in their school placements.

As we move into and through the next millennium, the story of teaching becomes more complex, more exciting, and more important. If you're looking for validation of what you are currently practising in your classroom; if you're searching for new ways to think about programming or for new ideas to blend into your day; if you're working with multi-age groups and are in need of organizational tips . . . this book is for you.

Enjoy your read!

Ron Benson
Toronto, Ontario
July, 1998

WHO WE ARE

Cecilia Taaffe
and
Barbara Szatañski

Marcel Proust once said, *"We don't receive wisdom; we must discover it for ourselves after a journey that no one can take for us or spare us."* We are teachers who continue to search for the best ways to serve children as educators. We don't have all the answers and we are always looking to make improvements. Perhaps the best thing that could have come out of our search so far has been to find each other and form our partnership.

Our journey together began while we were both studying towards a Master in Education degree concentrating in Psychopedagogy at the University of Ottawa. Discovering a definite synchronicity in our thoughts on learning and teaching, we worked towards a shared vision and managed to reach our goal of team teaching in a multiage setting.

Not only do we share a professional life, but we have much to say to each other about raising teenage children. There are delights and frights that have elicited many a laughter and tear throughout these years. We also share a strong desire to see the world and travel the continents.

We have had the pleasure of meeting many wonderful teachers while presenting at conferences, workshops, and university courses across Ontario, Quebec, and Newfoundland. We have published articles based on our experiences teaching in a child-centred and multiage classroom and have been co-editors and authors of The University of Ottawa Chapter of Phi Delta Kappa News/Nouvelles. We have been awarded the ***Phi Delta Kappa Award of Excellence*** for 1996 and 1997, as well as the ***Prime Minister's Award of Excellence in Teaching Math, Science, and Technology*** in 1997.

One of our goals now is to reach out to colleagues who are interested in creating dynamic classrooms of their own and to provide them with as many resources as possible. We are available for consulting and presenting workshops on the implementation of the concepts written in ***Classroom of Choice***. Meanwhile, we continue to work full-time as team teachers of a grade 2, 3, and 4 multiage class.

We are currently compiling and publishing a set of resources which support the implementation of the centres, systems, and projects discussed in ***Classroom of Choice.*** For inquiries regarding availability of these resources contact us at:

P.O. Box 41063,
Elmvale R.P.O.,
1910 St. Laurent Blvd.,
Ottawa, ON., Canada K1G 5K9
FAX (613) 248-3611
Phone (613) 248-3600
Toll free 1-877-49Cebra
or visit our website at www.cebra.anadas.com
or e-mail address: cebra@anadas.com

PREFACE

The last of the human freedoms —
to choose one's attitude
in any given circumstances,
to choose one's own way.
— VICTOR FRANKL

A Snapshot of Our Classroom

As you enter our dynamic classroom you are greeted by a busy hum of activity. The students are seated in clusters of work tables and activity centres set up around the room. The classroom has a large amount of learning materials. The walls and chalkboards are covered with information in the form of posters, charts, a calendar, graphs, lists, and pictures.

Some students are sitting on the floor with their work. Three are working just outside the open door into the hallway on a large scroll creating a time line of Canadian inventions. One is posting some of her self-chosen work to display it proudly on Our Writers' Wall.

A couple of students have chosen to work with pattern blocks and they are discussing how they can now transform their two-dimensional design into one that is three-dimensional. The overhead projector is being used to enhance the pattern block design. Elsewhere problems are being worked out using number charts and counting blocks.

A student is looking for resource material on the digestive system. She saw a television show on it and would like to know more so she can do a research report on that topic. She accesses information on the computer using a CD ROM and prints out data for future reference.

One table is filled with money. It is not the real kind but a good likeness of it. Students are working at the banking/money centre. They are on a shopping spree, using calculators to determine how much they have spent and then writing cheques to cover their costs. In the end they leave with a bit of "cash", the balance in their bank account.

A few students are at the audio centre. They have just heard some information on the deciduous forests of Canada while viewing a filmstrip, and are discussing how they will incorporate this information into a project. One has decided to make a poster that would display it. The other two are discussing how they could make it into a book on trees. They begin to work together on their writing. Two children are working on the computers quietly publishing their animal research projects. Another child sits at a small round table with the teacher, who is conferencing with her about her writing.

In the technology corner, several students are at the construction centre. They are collaborating on the design of a space ship with a detachable moon buggy. They are building it out of Construx blocks, writing up a report on their procedure, and illustrating their construction with a labelled diagram. One student would like to transfer this onto a poster at the poster project centre. Meanwhile, two girls are at the design-a-solution centre, and on paper are trying to determine the best ways to extricate a cat from a tree, and which tools would help solve the problem.

The VCR is playing a series of Canadian vignettes from the National Film Board for the students' critical analysis. Once the vignette is viewed students need to report some relevant information on the study of Canada. As well, students critique the video's presentation of information and consider possibilities of creating their own using this medium.

Two boys are working on the floor doing a long division problem and are excited to see that they already have gotten answers with six digits past the decimal point. Over at the science centre three girls are doing an experiment on light and prisms and excitedly call another over to see how they have "split" the light. One student busily writes a note to the librarian requesting books on space, then goes to a teacher to get it initialled, thereby receiving permission to go to the library. A few children are cozily curled up near the numerous books located in the class book resource centre.

At the side of the room two children are looking at the check-in system, deciding which activity to select next. All students are engaged in a variety of learning activities.

This dynamic classroom is not only a warm and inviting place to be, but is also exciting and stimulating for both students and teachers across the grades from primary to junior.

TABLE OF CONTENTS

INTRODUCTION

The shoe that fits one person pinches another;
there is no recipe for living that fits all cases.
— CARL GUSTAV JUNG

Years of being confronted with students' many needs and demands propelled us to create systems and materials which would be flexible but structured enough to serve these diverse needs. We wanted to be able to focus our teaching time on our students and our interactions with them rather than on developing new materials every time our grade assignment changed.

To begin with we took stock of the elements of teaching we believed were the cornerstones of a successful programme. We discovered the biggest underlying feature was choice. This came in the form of choice for both students and teachers. For students choice comes in so many areas and for teachers it is the choice to build a teaching model that really empowers learning.

We have written this resource guide for the design of a dynamic classroom which ties all the necessary ingredients of current pedagogy together. We hope it is as exciting for you to build your design of a dynamic classroom as it has been for us!

About this book

This book is written for the teacher who believes in choice. To have choice is to be empowered and to be empowered is to not only learn but <u>learn</u> to learn. It is written for the teacher who wishes to begin designing a dynamic classroom using our teaching model. If you are a teacher who believes in teaching children to become all that they can be during the time they spend with you, then this book is for you. It will provide you with the framework and resources to begin organizing your dynamic classroom. In this book you will find:

- a description of a dynamic classroom
- a basic understanding of the multiage setting
- a step-by-step approach to choosing learning centres and setting up a check-in system
- directions for how to plan and set up the physical classroom environment
- a how-to guide for organizing your class into heterogeneous learning groups
- a scheduling system for teaching and learning events
- a how-to guide for developing centres that can be used over and over again no matter the grade
- some daily classroom management and organization systems
- teaching strategies and authentic learning events
- daily tasks of which students are in charge
- assessment and evaluation methods which will enhance the learning dynamics
- a bibliography of recommended reading and support resources.
- blackline masters to support any of the strategies or systems discussed in the book

It is hoped that the teacher who begins this process of designing a dynamic classroom based on choice will wish to continue to develop her or his own ideas specific to his/her student population, environmental specifications, and community. It is not reasonable to expect to implement all that we outline in this book in one single year. It has taken us the better part of ten years to come up with it all and we are still refining it. It requires that in each successive year you build on the work of the previous one, by enhancing the number of learning centres, systems, and strategies already in place.

By beginning with a portion of what you see in this guide, you will have the necessary materials and blueprints to lay a solid foundation for building your own dynamic classroom, without being overwhelmed. It is recommended that you read this teachers guide from cover to cover first, as it was written with a holistic philosophy in mind. It is always beneficial to get the sense of the "bigger picture" before engaging in the step-by-step process outlined in this book. You will notice that some new terminology is presented in earlier chapters but not fully explained until later chapters. This is merely an organizational feature so that we can deal thoroughly with topics in their designated chapters. Wherever possible we refer you to the appropriate chapters for more information on a given term.

This book does not provide you with an extensive description of the theoretical underpinnings of our philosophy and teaching model. However, rest assured that this model was carefully constructed after extensive reading of the master theorists of our time, and those of the past. We are beholden to whole language theorists such as Ken and Yetta Goodman, Don Holdaway, Marie Clay, and Judith Newman, for a critical understanding of the need to address all learning holistically and with authenticity. We looked to the writing specialists Nancie Atwell, Frank Smith, and Donald Graves to refine our understanding of the writing process. Our philosophy also developed from the psychopedagogy various authorities such as Piaget, Erikson, Vygotsky, and Glasser espoused. Cognitivist and constructivist theories have influenced our outlook on learning and the resulting model we have designed. To embrace these theories and beliefs, we needed to make a paradigm shift away from the views of traditional teaching. We have provided you with a bibliography of recommended reading which will give you the background required to fully understand the components of the dynamic classroom. We urge you to take the time to do as much of the reading as possible as this will assist you in seeing the big picture in full colour.

What this book provides you with is a guide for how to organize and put into place systems that will facilitate learning. There are two main components: the explanatory text and the blackline masters.

The chapters of the text cover the basic philosophy and theory, the design of the classroom environment, the development of learning centres, assessment strategies, organization and classroom management, scheduling, and overall maintenance of the model. You are the professional who will still make choices about how to teach. This is a way to package your teaching in a model that will benefit your students.

The blackline masters support the strategies in management, organization, assessment, scheduling, and maintenance discussed throughout the text. These are located at the back of the book for reproduction.

Each step, system, and blackline master outlined in this book has been tested and retested in classrooms. Because of the holistic philosophy and theory, which are the basic underpinnings of the dynamic teaching model, we encourage teachers not to take bits and pieces from this book without being knowledgeable of the intended purpose and outcome of each. Each component is integral to the other, interconnected to comprise the intricate infrastructure of the dynamic teaching model. Once all is in place, it can be said that it seems to mesh together, much like the gears of a finely tuned piece of machinery.

The sequence of this book attempts to be logical as well as pragmatic, to maximize efficiency and productivity for teachers, at a time when demands are many and time is short. Take it one step at a time and you will build something that is exciting, rewarding and ever-changing, as children take charge of their learning.

....

Read on and you will notice how remarkably simple and logical our organizational systems and curriculum processes really are. That is not to say it is easy to do. Without embracing this set of beliefs about learning, these practices would seem to be complicated. However, in view of our goals for children, the step-by-step approach outlined in this guide is the logical means in achieving these objectives. You will be challenging students to become lifelong learners, preparing them for the 21st century, while continually challenging yourself in building a dynamic classroom.

Enjoy the voyage and good luck!

Cecilia &
Barbara

CHAPTER 1

WHY WE DO WHAT WE DO

The first step is believing in ourselves, understanding
that we are indeed smart, even if we aren't rich.
And the second is giving up the myths of power.
— GLORIA STEINEM

The questions we ask ourselves

From the beginning of our teaching careers, we have asked ourselves, "Why do we do what we do?" Not in the sense, "My gosh, we must be crazy to do this!" O.K. maybe sometimes we do say that. (Actually we recently gave a presentation entitled, "No, we are not crazy. We chose to teach a multiage grouping!") But we ask ourselves this question with respect to each particular item we wish to implement in our programme. For instance, if we are asking our students to all read the same novel then we ask ourselves why are we doing that? Is it possible we think it is more manageable? Is it important that all students cover exactly the same content? Perhaps we don't have enough other novels? Do we want to control the pace and sequence? These are all legitimate reasons but our own questions run more in the lines of this:

- How can we provide the most choice for students?
- How can we meet diverse needs and interests while empowering learning?
- How can we preserve dignity and respect individuals as having the power to think for themselves?
- What systems can be put into place that will give as much ownership to the students as possible and will result in independent effective learning?

Then we ask ourselves:

- What can we create that will be user-friendly and adaptable by students and teachers for years to come, whatever the grade level?

You can't count on teaching the same grade level year after year. You may be required to start in September with a new grade, new curriculum, and new expectations. As well if you are teaching multiage groupings, you definitely want resources that are flexible and reusable. You could consider us environmentally friendly educators; we believe in the 3R's - reduce, reuse, and recycle.

The goals we have for our students

The answers to the above questions are evident in this guide - an accumulation of open-ended, what we like to call 'generic' resources - classroom tested, and student-approved. We've made sure to get a lot of input and feedback from our students over the years. In fact, some of the modifications we have made are a direct result of their ideas. We've established a set of goals for our students which we aim to meet. These goals are:

- to be independent learners
- to have choice
- to be empowered (to have ownership of their learning)
- to preserve their dignity
- to be responsible for self and classroom
- to be critical and reflective thinkers
- to be decision makers and problem-solvers
- to be creative
- to meet or excel in the demands of an integrated, process-oriented skills
  practising curriculum
- to develop the multiple intelligences

With these goals in mind it is not implied that students are allowed to do as they wish. Students have choices within a framework and then are taught the expectations and consequences of those choices. As you will see, these are a set of complex and structured systems and expectations which work in concert with legislated curriculum, whatever the province or state you live in.

The goals we have for ourselves as teachers

As teachers and life long adult learners, we share the same goals that we have set for our students and we add the following:

- to have students be responsible for learning materials available to them
- to not take ownership of our students' learning
- to be organized within the classroom so students can follow through on being
  responsible
- to provide materials which challenge students at different ability levels
- to implement systems and create materials that incorporate the 3R's thereby
  reducing the stress load of teaching
- to allow for the most student-teacher contact as possible
- to treat students with respect and dignity

This is our shared vision and we believe we achieve these goals by implementing our model for the dynamic classroom.

CHAPTER 2

PREPARING STUDENTS FOR THE FUTURE

*I know of no more encouraging fact
than the unquestionable ability of man
to elevate his life by conscious endeavour.*
— HENRY DAVID THOREAU

Dynamic classrooms similar to those proposed by our model are a growing phenomenon in the world of schooling as we near the end of this century. The aim of schools is to prepare our students for the twenty-first century. What the future lives of our students will look like is very hard to predict, given the ever-increasing pace of change. The exact information and skills that students will need is also difficult to predict. As teachers, we therefore need to help our students become adaptable, independent problem-solvers who have the ability to gather any information needed, make sense of it, and present it in some way to others, or to use it to respond to the challenges in their lives.

Traditional classroom teaching models, i.e., teacher-centred models, have not consistently promoted independent, critical and creative thinkers, but have offered definitive outlines on what one must know. The dynamic class operates on the understanding that learning is not finite and is on-going throughout life, as people in the future are likely to have many careers during their lives. They will need to know how to be independent, adaptable, and how to respond to the challenges they will face in every day life. Our vision of the dynamic classroom responds to the dynamics of the future by providing an environment based on real life tasks that encourage students to become independent, empowered learners. Such learners will be better equipped to solve real-life problems, to use their own creative thinking, and to share their learning, thereby enhancing learning of the whole class and the success of society in the future.

How we define dynamic

We have created the dynamic teaching model in order to serve the needs of today's learners in preparation for the twenty-first century. It is a pedagogical delivery system which is malleable, fluid, and elastic enough to meet the changing needs of individual students.

Essentially "dynamic" means the opposite of static. Dynamic is defined as 'active, forceful, energetic, capable of giving a sense of power and transmitting energy' (The New Lexicon Webster's Dictionary). This is what we had in mind when creating our dynamic classroom. It is this energy, and sense of power over learning that the students exude when you step into this classroom.

The dynamic classroom is founded on the relationships between the **curriculum,** the **student** (with parental support), the **teacher,** the learning **environment,** and the ongoing **evaluation** of their interconnections.

Because all elements of the dynamic classroom are interconnected, any change in one element results in changes in the other elements. Imagine if the interconnections in Figure A below were comprised of elastic (those are the lines which run from environment to math, or from student to teacher, etc.). Changes would necessarily affect all elements of the model.

Interconnections of Classroom Learning

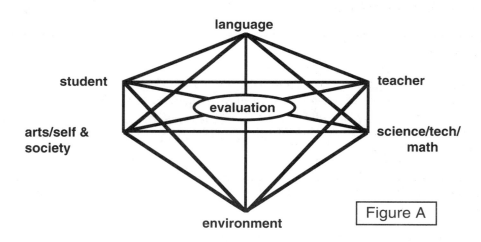

Figure A

Here is a simplified example. As a student learns the writing process in **language,** that will then affect how she or he can deal with researching and writing a project in the **science, math, or tech** area. It is more likely the student will take on the project with confidence, knowing the writing process. Then the **environment** must reflect the change towards the use of the writing process in the classroom by allowing for the necessary work space, and materials to follow through with all the steps of the writing process. In the meantime, the **teacher** must consider the types of teaching which would facilitate learning the writing process and consider methods of **evaluating** the student's progress and the programming appropriate to a process vs. solely product-driven curriculum. So you see the changes are far-reaching. No aspect of change will ever really occur in isolation.

Teaching practices in the dynamic classroom

Due to the nature of dynamic practices, change is a welcome process in such a classroom. Change is often relative to the amount of learning taking place. It is a classroom in which we, as teachers, have chosen to educate children using the following methods.

- a blend of child-centred and teacher-directed learning
- co-operative and collaborative learning

- learning through the multiple intelligences
- outcomes-based education
- an integrated, project-based, process-oriented curriculum using the inquiry approach
- an underlying structure which allows for student choice, decision-making, problem-solving, creative thinking, and responsibility
- active learning which includes a heavy emphasis on hands-on math, design and technology, and the sciences.
- multi-age teaching, continuous progress model
- developmentally appropriate practices
- a focus on literacy across the curriculum
- evaluation and authentic assessment

The roles of the student

We have expectations of our students. Those expectations imply that our students take on certain roles. Those roles entail that students will:

- respect other learners.
- demonstrate self-control.
- manage their time within the given limits.
- work co-operatively with others.
- respect the environment and conserve consumable materials.
- maintain the classroom organization and keep things in order.
- ask questions and search out answers.
- make suggestions and contribute ideas.
- negotiate modifications to activities.
- initiate projects to suit areas of interest.
- be responsible for their own learning by choosing to work at their appropriate developmental level.
- share their learning in a variety of ways.
- make choices that positively affect their learning.

The roles of the teacher

Within the dynamic teaching model, teachers also have roles that define what they do. The expectation is that teachers will:

- prepare and organize the classroom environment.
- provide learning activities that are in keeping with the dynamic teaching model's practices.
- act as facilitator and guide.
- plan learning activities and lessons to meet the requirements of the curriculum.
- communicate with parents.
- assess and evaluate students' learning.
- reflect on their own teaching practices, the curriculum, and the materials used within the classroom environment.
- make changes that will promote improvements to any of the interconnections
- offer choices to students.
- encourage and challenge students to refine their learning.
- provide daily feedback to students regarding their learning.
- give students frequent opportunities to communicate and share ideas.
- be clear and consistent about behaviour expectations.
- continually learn and challenge themselves.

For whom does this model work?

Teachers who choose to incorporate this design into their teaching practices will be allowing ample room for students to stretch to their greatest level of development. By providing an intricate infrastructure for students to have security and consistency in their learning, students are free to explore, take risks, and achieve maximum learning.

This design works for those who teach in single grade classrooms or in multiage classrooms but uphold the above-mentioned practices of a dynamic classroom. It is dynamic, flexible teaching practices which provide for optimal learning.

The dynamic teaching model is not exclusive to particular student populations. It has been used by French Immersion as well as special education teachers, ESL teachers, and regular English programme teachers. The model "fits" both primary and junior levels, but is not exclusive to them. Intermediate-level education currently promotes the kinds of teaching/learning practices espoused by those who use the dynamic teaching model to design their programs. The remarkably inclusive nature of this model welcomes and values the diversity that teachers accommodate in their classrooms every year.

The element of choice is a crucial one. It is important that teachers themselves decide to teach in this particular model. Teachers who embrace the philosophy of multiage practices from a deep-rooted belief in it are more apt to achieve a higher degree of success. These teachers are more likely to seek ways of bridging the gap between theory and practice.

Administrators can play a vital role in their support of such programs. They can encourage those who undertake the model in their schools as they will need to provide information and feedback to both teachers and parents on the efficacy of such a programme. They can provide important release time for teachers so that they can visit and talk with others who employ similar methods. They can also provide funding to attend conferences when topics are relevant to teaching in such an environment. These experiences proved invaluable to both of us when we were at the beginning stages of setting up our classroom. We were able to visually see similar classrooms and to clarify how the space might look, as well as talk to teachers who were kindred spirits, who provided the encouragement we needed.

Dynamic classroom practices lend themselves well to teaching in a multiage classroom. However, it is not necessary to adopt a multiage model in order to create a dynamic classroom. In the past, we have used all of the dynamic classroom elements while teaching a single grade and felt it was very valuable there as well. We will get into the added value of going with the multiage grouping in your classroom in Chapter 3: Why Choose Multiage?.

We have had the opportunity to use this delivery model in a multi-age setting in two schools. The schools are in neighbouring areas which serve a diverse population in which more than forty-four different cultural and linguistic heritages are represented. Many students are from low socioeconomic backgrounds. The schools both have many new Canadians. The class which we currently serve is representative of the school population, not specially selected to suit any specific requirements. We have taught groups of between forty-eight and fifty-four students from a variety of ability groupings and social backgrounds. Some of our students receive English as a Second Language support and others have been identified as learners with special needs. Specialist teachers in these areas work with us to include all students in the learning activities provided through this model.

The dynamic classroom, built on child-centred, activity-based, developmentally appropriate practices is a model that allows for the array of diversity found in groups of children of similar ages. It is rich in learning experiences, with abundant learning materials, with students who are challenged and prized for their uniqueness, while each contributes to the others learning.

Table 1 - page 18, Dimensions of Child Centeredness Assessed by the CCDS, was created for research purposes to assess the level of child-centredness in a sample of classrooms. We chose to include this table for reference because the elements of the scale clearly define what is required in a child centred classroom.

We have assessed our delivery of the model on these dimensions and the dynamic teaching model scores very high in child-centredness. If you develop a classroom which

The following table is reprinted by permission from *The Canadian Modern Language Review*.

Table 1
Dimensions of Child Centeredness Assessed by the CCDS
(Child Centered Dimensions Scale)

Direction

Students spend much time talking to each other, and to the teacher, to share information, clarify ideas, ask questions, and make suggestions. The classroom usually has a busy hum and the students are free to move around to achieve their goals. The teacher is a facilitator who provides assistance, encouragement, reassurance, and feedback. Questions are open ended challenges.

Physical organization

Work tables are usually set up in clusters, and are movable. Books and other materials, are available in various centers in the classroom. Bulletin boards are tied into the centers, displaying theme materials or various methods for recording student work choices. Work areas can include the halls, the library, and the school yard. Students contribute to decisions related to use of space.

Active learning

Students select real life problems which encourage the use of concrete materials as well as secondary sources of information. The students explore, question, predict, experiment, and seek the advice of peers and teachers. They formulate personal opinions about learning, based on the diversity of personal and cultural backgrounds. Students report and clarify learning to a variety of audiences, ;and peers and teachers are invited to challenge, question, and evaluate conclusions.

Subject integration

The timetable is divided into large blocks which are fluid and involve a minimum of major transitions. Activities begin without long waiting periods and involve thematic units or center work. Students are encouraged to describe their learning and to make connections with other curriculum areas.

Assessment/evaluation

Teacher observations are the basis for student evaluation. Observation takes places daily. The teacher uses anecdotal comments, conferences, work samples, and occasionally oral or written quizzes for assessment purposes. Student work is not red-penciled. Feedback to students is frequent. There is respect for the child's ownership of her or his work. Students' folders contain samples of their work, but not all work is expected to reach a final copy stage; hence work folders contain draft copies as well as finished work. Students are invited to use self-evaluation of how they are doing on a daily, weekly, monthly basis.

Choice

Students have freedom to choose, plan, and make decisions on topics, time, and format of their work. Activities are planned to require choices throughout the day. Student choices are encouraged and acknowledged by the teacher. Information about a student's work is recorded in a variety of ways, and samples of his/her work are chosen to reflect that student's ideas and purposes. Teachers help students prepare for schedule changes. They also encourage the view that teachers are learners alongside of students.

Curriculum flexibility

The teacher anticipates each child's needs for growth in skills, knowledge, and values. Community values are discussed. Experiences are provided that motivate students to solve problems and make decisions across the curriculum. Realistic expectations are set for students. Notebooks and work samples reflect a process of gradual refinement in which making mistakes and trying again is observable and predictable.

Initiative

When the teacher is interrupted or absent, work goes on. The students have planned what they are doing and take ownership of it. They often initiate activities. Students are encouraged to be risk takers and are encouraged to solve problems. Recess is sometimes viewed by the students as an inconvenient interruption.

Individualization

Modifications to meet individual needs are clearly evident in terms of content, process, and product. Materials are chosen to provide for a range of skill levels. Children are allowed to work at their own pace. Timelines are flexible. Activities allow for differentiation according to cognitive abilities and learning styles. Peers and parent volunteers assist students.

Language

Students are free to talk among themselves, to ask questions, and to seek answers from others. Conversations between the teacher and students occur frequently and are used to develop a range of thinking and social skills. The teacher asks many open-ended questions which follow the child's lead with regard to topic. Much written language is displayed and includes both student and teacher-made efforts.

Classroom management

Classroom rules for behaviour are generated with a high level of student input through such means as regular classroom meetings. Students are given responsibility for making choices for their own behaviour, and may experience a logical consequence for choosing poorly. The classroom atmosphere is relaxed, with evidence of cooperation and mutual respect. The focus is on the positive (e.g. good choices, meeting personal needs).

Global

The classroom is child centered. The focus is on creating optimum conditions for children's learning. The teacher searches for ways to enable each student to learn.

adheres to these dimensions then the twenty-first century should be a comfortable place to be for the children who are involved in such learning experiences.

We once had the opportunity to get some feedback from a class of grade 5,6 students who had been implementing the dynamic teaching model for about a year. When asked what they valued about this kind of learning, they replied without hesitation, "The opportunity to make choices among a variety of activity centres!" They appeared happy, eager to share their learning experiences, and motivated to help their teacher come up with more learning activities within the model. It was a highlight for us receiving such honest and uncensored reflections right from the participants.

•••••••••••••

In developing your model of the dynamic classroom you may want to consider the option of using a multiage setting. There are solid reasons why we have chosen it for ourselves. We discuss those reasons in the next section.

CHAPTER 3

WHY CHOOSE MULTIAGE?

*The essence of our effort to see that every child has a chance
must be to assure each an equal opportunity,
not to become equal, but to become different —
to realize whatever unique potential of body, mind
and spirit he or she possesses.*
—— *JOHN FISCHER*

We don't wish to promote the dynamic teaching model as exclusively suited to multiage but we have found that the multiage setting meets all the tenets of sound pedagogy to which we adhere. For that reason we have chosen to include some explanation of multiage practices in this book and let you decide for yourself whether the multiage model is something you would like to pursue.

A multiage class is defined as a class in which teachers have elected or chosen to educate children who vary in age by three or more years. In other words, children in two or more consecutive grades come together as a single unit.   This practice brings together groups of children of a consecutive age group to form what is also known as a family grouping. We have had siblings in our classes of 7, 8, 9, and 10 year olds in a grade 2, 3, and 4 class. The students are meant to enter at the grade 2 level and stay on for three full years. While we consider teacher choice to be crucial for success in undertaking to teach a multiage grouping, historically and currently teachers are sometimes required by administrators to teach children of two or more grades as a class. This is usually because there are not enough children of a particular grade to make up the required numbers for a class, so they are combined with part of another grade to make a class. Such a class is usually known as a split or combined grade.

The split grade/multiage difference

Split grades are very different from multiage classes, both in philosophy and in teaching and learning practices. In our experience we have observed that split grade teachers tend to treat each grade in the class as separate entities, often teaching to one grade while the other grade is given work assignments. Each grade uses different text books and is expected to learn a different curriculum. At times classes may be conducted as a whole but this is usually the exception and not the rule. In such a classroom the teacher is following the beliefs underlying the graded system.

The graded system is based on the belief that all nine year olds, for example, have very similar learning needs, learn in the same way, and are therefore best taught with other nine year olds. It is very much the factory model from beginning to end based on the idea that workers install similar components in the same way and at the same time. Time is monitored in discreet units and bells ring at specific times. When you've put in your time you move up to the next level. There is no pedagogical evidence for maintaining this model and yet it has been with us, in urban centres, for over one hundred years. The beliefs of the multiage system are very different. They are beliefs which are easily upheld by the teacher of the dynamic classroom.

These teachers accept each child as an individual with particular learning needs. Each child has arrived at their present understanding because of the way each child has processed his or her particular learning experiences. Parents and teachers know that no two children are alike, regardless of their age, that they rarely approach the same problem in the same way, and that they have their own unique interests, abilities, and talents.

Addressing different needs

Diversity is seen in any classroom, single graded or not. Some children in grade three are able to read at a grade six level, while others are still struggling with very easy early-read texts. We see children who are bored by the grade-level tasks in math, for example, because they have long ago mastered the skill required while others struggle with the most basic computations, and concepts. Grade level or age level curriculum expectations do not appear to fit the larger proportion of children. Children do not follow an exact rigid line of development. Unfortunately schooling practices have not traditionally allowed for the array of differences at any grade level.

The dynamic classroom does not need to follow the rather rigid, lock-step, time-based curriculum built upon age or grade expectations, but allows the curriculum to be matched more closely with the needs and abilities of each learner. It is driven by outcomes-based learning.

The dynamic classroom welcomes multiage groupings. Multiage groupings somewhat resemble family groupings or neighbourhood groupings. Today children are introduced very early in life to same age groupings. They often attend preschools and day care programs with same age children. They have very little time to interact with younger or older children. This trend continues on into school years. It denies children the opportunity to learn from children a little older, and denies them the experience of being leaders and experts to younger children. In the work force, more and more companies require employees to be team players and this is definitely not based on age. Children in a multiage group will work cooperatively with children of the same and other ages who have similar interests and abilities.

The dynamic classroom allows all children to be experts and novices at some time. In a traditional 'static' class, the more able or older children are usually always the leaders, while children who have not reached that level of development will often never have the opportunity to be in the role of expert or leader. For example, a child who is physically smaller or born in December may be considered by the other students to be the "baby" of the class. In a traditional class this role never changes, year after year. However, if a dynamic class incorporates the multiage model, it allows students to begin their first year as novices but by the next year or two they become the leaders to the new novices that enter their class.

Multiage groupings make a difference

Research tells us that there are many benefits to multiage learning. Anderson and Pavan (1993) summarized 64 research studies on nongraded, or multiage classes. This review indicated that 58% of children from multiage classes performed better than their peers on measures of academic achievement, 33% did as well, while only 9% did worse. Although academic achievement is certainly important, multiage classes seem to affect other factors of a students life. Pavan's review also indicated that students in a multiage setting were more likely to have positive self-concepts, high self-esteem, and good attitudes towards school.

We can personally attest to positive attitudes towards schooling. Our students, upon entering our class, will immediately check out their activity centre assignment for the day, bring their work to their table, get their school supplies assembled, and get to work, even before the announcements and official marking of the beginning of the day. These students not only come to school ready to begin their work, they often choose to stay during recess, to finish up a project or assignment. At lunch time children often negotiate time with us to conference a story or to work on the computer. If children are responsible enough to take on this extra time we rarely refuse the request, although occasionally we know we need a break and tell this to the student.

Children tell us they hate to miss school, and during a seasonal winter storm in Ottawa, we tend to have few absences relative to some other classrooms. During storms, the schools are usually kept open, but the school buses don't run. Therefore, many students have valid reasons to stay away. However, most of our students either arrange alternate rides to school or bundle up against the cold winds, and walk. If we ask them why they don't stay home they tell us they don't want to miss anything.

Building the confidence of parents

Parents in conversations with us, have often reported that they have noticed a change in their children's attitudes about school. They have told us that their child before this multiage classroom often said they felt sick on a typical school morning when it was clear they were not, in order to stay at home. Once in the multiage classroom, they no longer have these 'tummy' aches. Some have told us of children who were fearful and very anxious about school, until they have joined the multiage class. We think that for many children who are given options and choices and respect as learners, the anxiety school can foster diminishes and they just want to get on with the interesting things they are doing. It is obvious these children feel good about their learning.

One of the concerns parents often share with us is that while they can see the benefits to younger children learning and working with older children, they assume that the older child will somehow miss out in this environment, and not be as challenged. We have noticed otherwise. What we see is that children who have to explain something to someone else, have to refine and review the information they have learned in order to teach it to someone else. This is what teachers seem to experience as well as they refine and review material they teach. Children become stronger in the knowledge they share and are able to move on to more advanced learning.

The multiage classroom accommodates the developmental needs of learners better than a straight grade class in many ways. Older students and more able students are encouraged to take on fuller, in depth studies of a topic or area of learning, and the less able, older students can join the middle of the group to review or learn what they need most. Younger children, who can do so, can join older students if they are ready for this. This moving in and out of groupings is unobtrusive and children become comfortable finding the place that suits them.

Because students stay with the same teachers for two or three years the relationship with parents becomes even more critical. To build this relationship it is well advised that teachers have a meeting with parents very early in the school year to tell them about the class set up, its benefits, the expectations, what they will see coming home, how they can help at home and in school, and how they become a very important part of their child's learning experience. We have found that such a meeting usually wins over some new and skeptical parents to the group. Our greatest advocates are the parents of the children we teach. They usually will attest to the benefits they have seen their child gain. During our meeting the experienced parents usually dispel the fears and anxieties of the newly initiated. Communication with parents becomes easier with each passing year as we develop a stronger relationship with them. We usually get to know the child and the family fairly well. We build on that family relationship and usually have siblings join us when they are of age. Sometimes we are working with the same parents for five or six or more years. As this relationship grows, parents really begin to see themselves and teachers as members of the same team. They become much less confrontational and approach any problem as a joint challenge.

Parents are a great resource of talent and energy and without them our programme would have many more bumps in the road. They have given of their talent to demonstrate or teach. Volunteer parents give their time to have students read to them, conference a story or help organize resources for a project. They have collected materials so we could reuse them in creative ways. For example,we have received out-of-date office supples from parents, address labels, paper of all kinds, envelopes, packaging materials that eventually became lap desks, and many recycled resources that are used in the technology centres, and so on. They have made rough draft booklets, photocopied materials, and prepared and laminated materials for the centres. They have cut, trimmed, coloured, collated, stapled and labelled for our students. Parents support our programme in so many ways. We cannot thank them enough.

Everyone benefits from the multiage continuous progress model

As students continue with us for more than one year, this allows the teacher-student relationship to grow. The children become more confident in approaching us with an idea or question. They are not anxious about beginning the second year with us as we are familiar to them and there is a level of comfort already established. They join the nucleus of students who are knowledgeable about the classroom layout, the set-up, and the systems we employ. We rely on the experienced students to be responsible for and maintain these systems while the new-comers learn them.

We know the returning students from day one in any given year and we know where they are as learners. It doesn't take us several weeks or months of observations and assessment to determine their developmental level. They can usually pick up where they left off in the continuum of their learning. They do this literally as well as figuratively. Often a child will pick up their writing folder on the first day back, see a rough draft story they were working on in June and set right to work to finish it. Parents tell us returning to school is very easy, both for the child and the parents as they both know what to expect.

Research supports a multiage approach in education. For further reading on this topic, refer to the Multiage Teaching section of our bibliography. Our own experience tells us that this added dimension to a dynamic classroom betters the education and development of our students.

A word of caution regarding the multiage approach is that it requires more work and flexibility of programme and practitioners. We have learned that having a partner is a great built-in support system. We also know we have to say when we have reached our limit or when we need to hang back on starting some new initiative because we don't have the energy or time. We know that our own mental and physical well-being must be nourished too, so that we can revitalize ourselves, and fight against burnout. Unless support is there, optimism, energy and creativity would be very difficult to maintain. While setting up and running your dynamic classroom, ensure that you do the things that you need to do to recharge your batteries.

With this balanced approach we can't imagine teaching in any other way. Not only are students happy in this classroom, the teachers are too. Ultimately, the joy of learning of both teachers and students is why we choose to teach in a multiage classroom, in a dynamic teaching model.

Whether you choose to teach in a multiage setting or not, there are a number of things you can do to develop the dynamic teaching model in your class. The first step is to choose the learning outcomes you want to achieve with your students and the corresponding centres. Centres make up about one quarter of our day. They provide a focal point for much of our teaching beyond activity centre time.

CHAPTER 4

THE FIRST STEP

Decide what you want, decide what you are willing to exchange for it.
Establish your priorities and go to work.
— *H.L. HUNT*

Choosing the centres

Once you have decided that the dynamic teaching model is for you, the first step is to make a plan. The plan begins with choosing the learning outcomes which you wish to achieve in your classroom. After you plan what it is that you expect the students to achieve in their learning, you pick the centres which will best accommodate the learning expectations you have. (In Chapter 7: Learning Centres, we list all the centres and the intended expectations for each.) For example, we wanted to make sure that we addressed all the multiple intelligences through our centres. There are seven intelligences as defined by Howard Gardner (1983). They are:

· spatial/visual
· linguistic/verbal
· intrapersonal
· musical/rhythmic
· bodily/kinesthetic
· interpersonal
· logical/mathematical

Therefore we have included a music centre, dance centre, and personal well being centre, as well as centres that utilize the academic intelligences students apply in the maths, sciences, and language.

Plan for all the centres you wish to implement. You will probably find that a year is not long enough to implement all that you had planned. For example, at the beginning of a school year we added a new centre to our list, like the newspaper centre or the consumer affairs centre, only to take a whole year to open it. Sometimes it is necessary to allow for the right circumstances to surface before you open a new centre and provide all the necessary materials to go with it. It may take one or two students to see a centre label, make an inquiry about it and then we decide to open that centre. Choosing what goes in the centres and when they are to be open is further explained in Chapters 7 and 12 respectively.

Let your imagination run wild when designing centres and then come back down to reality and fine tune your choices. Consider starting small but nonetheless choose at least one centre from each area of learning.

Don't let yourself fall into the trap of naming centres too specifically, which may have you scampering for ideas to put into those centres. In one of our early years we fell into that trap and had a geoboard centre, a pattern block centre, a crossword puzzle centre and so on. We soon found out that those types of activities could have been accommodated in a math blocks centre and a spelling/word study centre, which also left us open to putting a myriad of other activities in those centres when we saw the need. Don't limit yourself by choosing only language arts centres when you know that down the road you will want to have math and science type centres as well. What you begin with in your planning sets the tone for the whole year and gives you goals to work towards. By choosing the outcomes for the whole year, you are really choosing the centres and you are beginning the first step in the design process.

You will find detailed information for designing the centres to meet your specific classroom needs, in Chapter 7: Learning Centres, as well as some background information, and suggested resources.

The element of choice plays a key role throughout the development of your own dynamic classroom. As you develop more confidence and understanding of a complete and integrated curriculum provided through the open-ended learning tasks set out in learning centres, you will begin to see that the possibilities are endless. Our suggested list of centres is not intended to be comprehensive. It is hoped that you will be inspired to create learning centres which are tailored to the specific needs of your students. As the teacher, you are the expert regarding the educational needs of your students. You decide where you want to make changes and adaptations. Our model provides a framework in which you can create your own dynamic classroom. Flexibility is a built-in feature of the dynamic teaching model which encourages individual design models. Photocopy the Blackline Master #7 Centre List for the Year in which to record your choice of centres, and make the list of centres you plan to begin with. On the following page is our current list from which we are operating, along with our total list of possible choices. Our purpose for each centre is explained in Chapter 7: Learning Centres so read on before you make any final decisions about choosing centres.

It is a good idea to begin thinking of your centres as soon as you know your assignment in May or June for the following year. Once you have made your list of possible centres, keep this list handy as you are in the developing process because you may come across ideas and resources during the intervening time, which will be appropriate for specific centres.

A broad range of centres are suggested to cover most curriculum areas. Some centres are more suitable for primary grades and others are intended for the upper primary, junior and intermediate grades. Many of them are adaptable to all grades. Since we view language, the arts, personal development, science, technology, and math as interconnected it becomes important to develop a curriculum that is integrated and multi-dimensional. The dynamic teaching model facilitates this kind of curriculum design.

Start small but do it right

Unless you want to feel, on the first day of school, that a herd of buffaloes is attacking the beautiful centres that you have so painstakingly prepared during the summer or previous year, we advise you to start small. Once both you and the children have adapted your learning to the use of centres, then you can begin to develop and build the other centres that you wish as the year progresses and in the following years.

When we began using centres we chose to use a small number. By the end of the first year, we had about twenty-five centres functioning in a primary grade. Each year we learned how to manage centres better and built up our resources. We came to understand the tremendous value of teaching through centres so it was logical to add a few more. Now we are operating from a base of about fifty-two centres. It is possible to combine the curriculum ideas of several centres under one name in order to cut down on the maintenance of numerous centres. This can be done for example by combining Construction, Technology Tools, and Design-a-Solution

Our complete list of centre choices

- animal research
- art
- audio
- banking/money
- big books
- board games
- book/resource
- calculator
- calendar
- Canadiana
- chalkboard
- computers
- construction
- consumer affairs
- cooking
- correspondence
- cursive writing
- dance
- design a solution
- drama
- drawing
- ecology
- experiments
- film projector
- flannel board
- grammar examiner
- history
- inventions
- journal writing
- make-a-book
- magnetic board
- map and globe
- math
- math blocks
- math games
- math problems
- measurement
- media
- music
- newspaper
- novel study
- overhead projector
- paint easel
- personal well-being
- poetry study
- poster projects
- publishing centre
- puzzles
- research projects
- sand table
- science
- sculpture
- shared reading
- spelling
- story study
- story writing
- tape recording
- technology
- technology tools
- toys
- video
- water table
- weather

Centres for the Year

- animal research
- art
- banking/money
- big books
- board games
- book/resource
- calculator
- calendar
- Canadiana
- construction
- consumer affairs
- correspondence
- cursive writing
- dance
- design a solution
- drama
- drawing
- ecology
- experiments
- grammar examiner
- history
- inventions
- journal writing
- make-a-book
- map and globe
- math blocks
- math games
- math problems
- measurement
- media
- audio
- film projector
- overhead projector
- video
- music
- newspaper
- novel study
- paint easel
- personal well-being
- poetry study
- poster projects
- publishing centre
- puzzles
- research projects
- science
- sculpture
- shared reading
- spelling
- story study
- story writing
- technology tools
- weather

under the Technology Centre. This will make more sense to you as you read the descriptions of the centres in Chapter 7: The Learning Centres. There you will recognize other centres that could be amalgamated under one heading. In the beginning we were careful to pick a small group of core centres that represented all of the learning strands.

For example, for the learning strands of Math, Science, and Technology we chose:
Math Problems, Math Blocks, Science, Computers, Audio, Overhead, Technology Tools, Design-a-Solution, Construction Centre, and Puzzles.

In the area of Language we chose:
Correspondence Centre, Book/Resource Centre, Story Writing, Spelling, Grammar Examiner Centre, Make-a-Book Centre, and Journal Writing.

For The Arts we chose:
Drawing Centre, Art Centre, Paint Easel Centre and Drama Centre.

For Self and Society we used:
Canadian Trivia Centre, and Map & Globe Centre.

Make choices based on your own comfort zone and what you would like to try first.

There are pragmatic decisions to make as well. You may well have to consider the resources that are available to you. We have learned over the years that there are lots of great resources that can be easily adapted for use in learning centres. With little effort and time on our part, we were able to incorporate that material to be used in a way that supported the elements of student choice and ownership of learning. It took us a while to understand that we did not have to design every single element of a centre if there already existed great resources that served our centres well.

Consider the centres as a means for exploring, developing, and reinforcing skills in language, the arts, self and society, science, technology and math. They are not designed as "extras" for after the "real work" is done. A portion of each day is set aside for centre time (See Chapter 11: Scheduling). During centre time, students are actively engaged in choosing centres, and in real learning. Students see this as the most vital part of their day. They arrive at school eager and ready to begin.

In our classroom most children do not wait for the morning announcements and "Oh Canada" as a signal to begin their day. As soon as they arrive they begin with checking in and moving right to their centre work. Occasionally, through a special assembly or some unexpected interruption we have had to announce a 'no centre' day. The children groan with disappointment. They are so eager to complete their centres that they are unhappy with such interruptions.

When you start to plan, consider which centres you can carry through the whole year in a variety of ways. They are not meant to be specific to a particular theme and only carried out for a month. This does not mean, however, that you must have every centre operating without fail every day of the school year. Once centres are up and running you will set a series of must-do centres to ensure that your students cover prescribed curriculum areas.

Over the years the idea of having students complete a daily required centre became more and more useful to us. With this requirement we can ensure the students go to a variety of centres and that all areas of the curriculum are being addressed. This rotation system is always seen as equitable and therefore there is never anyone who balks at the idea of going to a particular centre. Once the child has completed this required daily centre, she/he can then go to any centre of her/his choice as long as it is 'open', and she/he will know that if a ticket is in the pocket it is available and open to her/him. We call this series of required centres "must-do centres". Some teachers do not have must-do centres. They allow children to set up their contracts of centre choices. You as the facilitator decide how children will work through the centres.

There is a system which allows you to open and close centres throughout the year based on curriculum needs. (See Chapter 6: The Check-in System.) Keeping a centre operational may be easier than you realize. Keep reading and you will find out how easy it really is.

CHAPTER 5

THE LEARNING ENVIRONMENT

Every cubic inch of space is a miracle.
— *WALT WHITMAN*

What we plan we build.
— *PHOEBE CARY*

We couldn't decide whether you would need to begin with choosing the learning centres first or with the actual set-up of your classroom. It is one of those chicken and egg dilemmas. The type of physical space you have available to you could determine the centres you choose. In the end we decided that you do indeed need to have the bigger picture in your head - i.e. the centres you want to implement, before transforming the physical space into the classroom environment you envision. We have done so in a variety of classroom spaces, from a portable classroom, to a small four-walls-and-nothing-else classroom, to a non-traditional classroom with pillars and angled walls, then to a brand new take-it-from-scratch classroom. You have to mould the space to suit what you want to happen there. "If you build it they will come."

What the dynamic classroom looks like

What makes a classroom environment inviting to learners? Any classroom can have desks, chairs, books, and an assortment of materials. How these things are arranged within the space of four walls can make the difference between a dynamic, vital, exciting, stimulating learning environment and a classroom which is simply a confined space.

From a single glance into a dynamic classroom, which is designed to enhance developmentally appropriate practices, an observer will view a variety of differences from the traditional classroom. There are no rows of individual desks carefully placed an equidistance apart. There is no teacher's desk at the helm of the classroom. Blackboards are not kept free and clear. Bulletin boards are not precisely arranged to display only the best of the students' work. Rather, what one will note is an intricate layout of tables and furniture fashioned to invite co-operative, collaborative, or independent learning.

Start with a large open area for whole class meetings

Central to the dynamic classroom design is the meeting area, usually an open carpeted area, which allows enough space for all the students to gather together. This space should be located where there is easy access to a blackboard or chart paper. This way you or the students can record information important to the meeting. On occasion, we have had to delineate the meeting area with masking tape to keep the group from sprawling out under the surrounding tables. We have found the closer the group can be to the speaker the easier it is for students to maintain eye contact, and the more likely it is that you will have everyone's attention. Not long ago, teaching partners at one of our workshops told us of a set of carpeted steps that were built to allow the back two rows of students to sit elevated while at the meeting. They were made of plywood just like you would build two steps, but a little deeper for sitting on, and covered over with comfortable carpeting. We have yet to take on that project, but it sounds like a workable solution to the problem of losing the attention of the furthest members of your audience.

The whole class needs to meet frequently to discuss decisions which will affect the entire group, and to obtain new information relevant to their learning. If you are team-teaching in a shared space, it would be prudent to provide for a second, smaller meeting area in the layout. We have found this second meeting area to be useful because there is always a need to discuss something with another group with different needs at some point in each day. This second space is used by one of us for small group mini-lessons while the remainder of the class is meeting with the other on another topic in the central meeting area. We often flip flop the use of the smaller area so one person is not feeling relegated to the smaller space all the time. It is convenient to have access to another writing surface in this second meeting area as well. If you can't swing getting a large wall-mounted whiteboard or chalkboard, there are the chart stand versions which make feasible alternatives.

Include table groupings which accommodate the whole class

Dispersed throughout the room, beginning around the meeting area, are table groupings. Hexagonal, round, or desks grouped together can be used for these purposes. We have a maximum of six students sitting at these groups. Students, regardless of age, work in groups at these tables when they are in need of such a space. Often older students can be found tutoring younger students thereby reinforcing their own learning. Table groupings are conducive to collaborative efforts. It also makes it easy for you to gather a small group together at a table to give a specific lesson. It is recommended that enough table groupings are made to fit the entire class. There may be instances when it is suitable for each student to have a place at a table. We sometimes do have all students writing something in their learning logs at the same time, or taking down a science note, or brainstorming on a topic. Inevitably there are those who still wish to move to the carpet and get closer to the board. The central floor space is the best location for the table groupings, in proximity to the meeting area and in view of some blackboard space.

Locating permanent centres

Around the perimeter of the room are clusters of bookcases, tables, and shelves designed to function as **learning centres.** Over the years we have scrounged every bit of furniture we could get our hands on. There isn't much that we can't put to good use. We currently have a small sofa in the book/resource centre, an old low dresser for dress up clothes, milk crates stacked to make bookshelves, an old TV stand for our big books and a variety of other shelving. Our husbands no longer blink an eye when asked to come to a screeching halt at a neighbour's discarded belongings or when asked to cart home a display rack from a liquidation sale while travelling on holidays.

We give a selection of main centres a somewhat permanent home in our classroom. These main centres include science, book/resource library, technology, audio, film projector, overhead projector, writing/publishing, mathematics, construction, painting, and art. Each centre has, accessible to the students, a variety of materials related to each area of learning. We don't get carried away and put everything we have in supply out for general use because before you know it things get into disarray. We keep a storage cupboard or two for the overflow and take things out only as they are needed. Materials are in labelled containers, and each container has a specific location for storage. The location is also labelled, so it is easy to find where something goes when it is taken out for use. This design is student user-friendly. The care and maintenance of the classroom lies on the students' shoulders. With that responsibility comes decision-making and problem-solving. Students are given opportunities to make choices, be creative thinkers and initiate collaborative projects, and have the resources they require available at their fingertips. In this way there is less chance you will be interrupted to assist someone with a gopher request.

Each centre location and design is chosen to maximize the probability of students to achieve desired outcomes. For example, the science centre is best located near windows where light will play a major role in observation and experimentation. Whether it is in growing specimens or carefully examining an item, light is an important factor in the exploration of science. The science centre needs a work surface and the necessary tools for exploration such as magnifiers, microscopes, trays, magnets, etc. Information books, experiment books, and writing supplies can be located here for easy access.

The math centres will need access to a number of shelves to store the numerous types of manipulatives often used in a hands-on math approach. The audio centre will need to be located near a wall plug and have enough room so that six students can sit around with headphones for each one. The overhead and film projector are always a challenge to find the right space for because you need both a wall plug and space on the wall to project the images. The film projector doesn't require a large image space and the overhead only needs a slightly larger space when only a small group is viewing the materials.

Our construction centre is housed in bins with roller wheels so that they can be easily carted to a large open space for collaborative construction. The art and painting centres are best located closest to a sink, on bare floor, and near some storage cupboards to keep paints, paper, and supplies handy. Sometimes our art table doubles as the technology centre when sawing, cutting, or gluing is involved because of its ease in clean-up. Each centre location is well thought out and has a direct bearing on the students' learning and the smoothness of the whole operation. The more efficiently each centre is organized, the less possibility there is for distraction. Students will expend minimum time and energy on unnecessary movement about the room.

Central in importance to our classroom is the book/resource centre. Because our own children are grown we have been able to stealthily remove most of their reading material from our homes and have it reside in our class library which we have called the book/resource centre. Both fiction and non-fiction reading material is available in this centre. It consists of all manner of print resources such as:

- magazines - e.g., Ranger Rick
- student published books
- picture books
- information cards
- novels of all kinds
- Audubon Nature Encyclopedia

- newspapers - local, kids, environmental
- comic books
- non-fiction books
- information brochures
- young children's science books
- World Book Encyclopedias

Another source of books is getting students to purchase from the publishers' book clubs from which the class earns free books based on student purchases. Whatever the source, we believe you can never have too many good quality books in the book/resource centre.

The book/resource centre is best located in a corner where a quiet reading space can also be provided. If you don't have a natural corner available, bookcases or other furniture can be used to section off a space. Books are organized and labelled so that each book can readily be returned, even by the youngest students, to its given location. Any categorization system which suits the teacher and students can be applied with the labelling system. We generally have non-fiction books together by topic and fiction books together either by related theme or challenge level. We keep classic picture books together and award winning books together. We also have some books categorized by author when we have enough of one author to fill a box. We mostly use magazine boxes purchased at any business supply store or discount department stores. The magazine boxes are handy because during whole class quiet reading time we can avoid a huge onrush of forty-eight students to the relatively small book corner by dispersing the magazine boxes full of books to different locations in the room for selection. Each book within a box has an identifying sticker on the back upper right hand corner. Then the magazine box has the corresponding sticker label. We started out with coloured circles, large and small, easily found at business stores as well. When the coloured sticker combinations were exhausted we turned to our treasury of shape stickers - shells, pumpkins, blue ribbons, etc. The shelf where each magazine box is kept also has the corresponding sticker label so there is no confusion in returning the boxes to their proper location. It is easy to see when something is misplaced or missing. Also, the wear and tear on books is reduced considerably when they are given the same home every day.

Secondary to the hub of activity at the book/resource centre is the publishing centre, better known as "Houston Central". We are lucky enough to have four computers which are networked to the school system and therefore have access to numerous programmes and the Internet. We have located these computers in a sort of U-shaped area right next to the writing centre so paper, publishing materials, book covers, dictionaries, and addresses are close by. The only thing missing is a printer. We have a central location for that in another room. Ideally, it would be located here as well.

Create a storage system for portable centres

All other centres which we call our portable centres are simply housed in the Rubbermaid™ type washbasins; sturdy, affordable and long lasting. They are given labels and a shelf-space so they are easily found. That is of course if they are put back after being used. (And we admit that doesn't always happen!) Many of the bins can be stacked on top of each other, about three high, to conserve space. We find it useful to have the shelf space labelled as well so that one can see at least where the bin is supposed to be.

Posting information and visual materials

Wall, bulletin board, and blackboard spaces are used to display charts, posters, maps, and word lists. These much needed resources are made visible for students to incorporate into their learning tasks. This information is a combination of student and teacher generated material directly related to the current topics of discussion. As much as possible, the needed information is displayed closest to the centre for which it is to be applied. Published writing is included in the class resource library, shared with other classes, or displayed in the principal's office. Each student is provided with a personal display space on "Our Writers' Wall". Individuals decide which works will be showcased and for how long. Artwork is included in published books, taken home, or hung in the gallery space for everyone to enjoy. The casual observer may see a lot of clutter but each visual aide is a necessary learning scaffold for the students.

············

This classroom, filled with students at various locations in the room, is a hive of activity. Students are talking, sharing ideas, sometimes moving from one spot to another but above all, learning. Can children not learn within any four walls, with a teacher, and the right lessons? Probably, but the difference is these children are happy, enthusiastic learners who are eager to experiment and initiate projects. They willingly take on challenging tasks and stick to them for days, ecstatic with their success upon completion. Naturally, it is the child-centred holistic philosophy behind the classroom design which drives this teaching model. The environment has a powerful effect on what goes on within these four walls. Careful thought and analysis of the placement of each centre and the materials that each student will require, will ensure an environment that respects the unique learning needs of each child.

This discussion of what the classroom space looks like gives the flavour of the very active real-life tasks of learning in which the students will engage. For many teachers who wish to implement such a model there is a feeling of being overwhelmed about where and how to begin. Some teachers want to dive right in while others prefer to implement the changes more slowly as their time, resources, and energy permit. Finding a kindred spirit can allow teachers to share resources, ideas, and be supportive to each other. They can even share teaching space, in a team teaching set-up, or allow students to have frequent visits to each others' rooms. The exciting adventure of teaching in such a dynamic classroom depends to a great deal on how you shape the environment.

Planning and preparing the learning environment

Teachers face numerous tasks every year before their new class can be welcomed. Teachers who wish to create dynamic classrooms have the task of deciding how best to utilize the space provided in order to set up effective activity centres, accessible resources and materials that stimulate independent learning and problem-solving.

For teachers who use the learning centre model, one of the first jobs is to plan which centres would best respond to the array of students they will receive and how best to maximize the space and materials provided. Learning centres which house the materials and resources for a particular curriculum area work well when set up around the perimeter of the room so the group work tables can then be placed in clusters in the centre of the room.

The challenge in setting up every classroom is to make everything in the space promote the behaviours and learning outcomes which are desired. It helps to keep clearly in mind the question, "what would happen if I place a particular object in a particular place ?" We need to think about such things as how a placement serves the students, will it cause congestion in an area, or will the placement of an object stimulate or promote the desired type of activity and learning outcome. Students in an activity-based, child-centred classroom who employ developmentally appropriate practices are encouraged to be independent problem-solvers. Part of real life decisions are deciding which resources are relevant to the project or activity at hand. Therefore, resources need to be accessible and to be well organized to promote such independent problem-solving. It also saves teachers many steps if students are responsible for taking care of their materials. Students feel empowered when they can make decisions which will affect their learning.

The dynamic class is alive and growing, so that even with the best planning and anticipating consequences, there are always going to be some placements of materials that will not work. Some adjustments and refinements will be necessary once the students actually try out the space.

Teachers, as much as the other learners in their class, are unique in their approach in solving every problem and task. Therefore, the following steps are suggestions on how one can plan, organize and implement the set-up of their dynamic classroom environment.

Steps in planning and organizing the dynamic classroom

We have ten steps that we follow whenever we begin a new classroom set-up.

(1) Organize the students in your class in groups of four to six.

(2) Review the activity centres you want to use for the whole year and list them.

(3) Draw a map of your room.

(4) Consider constraints and benefits created by the physical properties of a classroom.

(5) Move the tables, chairs, bookcases and other furniture.

(6) Move all the student materials to accessible locations.

(7) Give everything a specific spot and label it.

(8) Label and designate the working space for centres-in-a-tub.

(9) Display visual materials appropriate to the learning area.

(10) Designate wall space in and near the classroom for children to display their work.

These steps are given more detail in the following explanations:

(1) Organize the students in your class in groups of four to six.

By placing four to six students in each work group, an organizational tool is always in place. During activity centre time each group in our class is given a required or "must do" centre each day. (This strategy is described in detail in Chapter 8: Classroom Management and Organization.) Each child completes any unfinished projects or work, and can then freely choose any other centre which is opened. During other times in our day, this group sits and works at their designated group table. Each group is identified by the group centre symbol. We use geometric shapes such as circles, squares, triangles, hexagons, pentagons, etc. Each group table is labelled by a large shape which is hung above it. These groups are not set in stone for the whole year. Periodic changes are made and sometimes students make specific requests to have their assigned group changed. Regardless of belonging to a specific learning group, students will often work in different group configurations throughout the day depending on the focus of the work. Some of these groups work better when based on common interests, some need to be similar in ability, and yet others can be founded on social criteria, or the need to have some strengths mixed with weaknesses. However, for basic management needs we have found using groups with an identifiable name to be useful.

(2) Review the activity centres you want to use for the whole year and list them.

Look at the whole list of possible centres and choose the ones that you wish to incorporate at some point throughout the year. As the school year gets up and running, each learning group is given required centres to work on each day. Once the required work is completed students may choose other centres. As we continue to refine our thinking we have added and deleted some centres each year. But basically, as outlined in Chapter 4, we have a variety of centres that attempt to cover each curriculum area. Further details about the learning centres is provided in Chapter 7.

(3) Draw a map of your room.

After deciding which centres we wanted, we drew a map of our room, made several copies and began to place our permanent centres on the map. Take into consideration the factors mentioned above that each permanent centre requires and this will ease your decision-making. As windows and electrical outlets cannot be moved, some decisions are based on existing features of the environment. Making a floor plan on paper is an invaluable planning tool that allows you to try out several possibilities before actually moving anything. (Hint: Your class floor plan is probably easily available on the posted fire exit plan. Get a copy and enlarge the required classroom on your photocopy machine. Make several copies to work on.)

(4) Consider constraints and benefits created by the physical properties of a classroom.

Some decisions on placement of centres and all other materials are constrained by the physical properties of a classroom. One of our first classrooms had a large science lab type counter which was a permanent fixture at the back of the room. So we decided to get rid of the large, space gobbling teachers' desks and converted the countertop to our own personal desk space complete with science lab stools! This is just a small example of the need to tailor your classroom to existing characteristics. Many of these pragmatic elements will influence the flow of the classroom and the follow through of the class's learning.

We needed the large shelf at the side wall to store all math manipulatives where they would be easily accessible to all the children. A large area near one of the chalkboards for large group meetings and instruction was also required. We had to set our listening centre near one of only two outlets in the room. The painting and art centre logically should be set up as near to the sink as possible for easy mixing of paints and clean ups. The activities related to reading, topic research, writing, and publishing of poetry, stories, and reports would be better served in the far corner where there would be less traffic and children would then have quieter work conditions with fewer distractions. The computers had to be located at the second set of outlets and as near the reading and writing activities as possible.

The large bright corner window provided space and light for nature and science projects. Because science and technology are related we felt the technology tools and table could work nicely near the science materials as well.

(5) Move the tables, chairs, bookcases and other furniture.

Our next step was to actually move the tables and book shelves, and except for some minor adjustments, we felt that planning done with the classroom maps had served us well. It made it much easier to know where things would be exactly placed.

(6) Move all the student materials to accessible locations.

After physically moving the basic furniture, such as tables, bookshelves, and computer tables, and placing them so as to separate the space into small discrete learning centre areas, we took on the task of moving all the student materials. We found that by working on one centre at a time we could keep our focus on the materials needed and complete one whole centre area before moving on to another centre. In our programme we make almost all materials available to our students, so that they are empowered to take control of as much of their everyday decisions and responsibilities as possible. Self-sufficiency is therefore promoted as well as efficiency. When students have the right to access materials and to be responsible for them, they are more efficient and teachers also do not waste precious moments passing out papers, rulers, markers, and other resources. Students in such an environment, need to have access to materials and need to know what is available so that they can make the best possible choices when solving their problems.

(7) Give everything a specific spot and label it.

Every resource was given a specific spot. Tubs that held materials were clearly labelled and a corresponding identical label was put on the shelf where it was placed. This makes it easy for each child to know where to return materials. A quick glance by a monitor or teacher can spot something misplaced and can call on the child who last used the equipment to return it to its place. Continuity and order are important for children to help reduce their frustration and allow them to get on with their jobs.

We store the job or task cards and material relevant to each centre in a tub clearly labelled by its centre name and by its graphic. Sometimes because the lack of space makes it impossible to set up all the desired centres in a fixed location, a tub becomes a centre which holds the required tasks or choices and materials offered at that centre. Children can then move that tub to a work area that is available.

(8) Label and designate the working space for portable centres.

Students get straight to work when they know where to access the materials and where they can set up their work. While many centres are permanently set up in a specific location and defined by tables, bookcases and so on, there are far too many centres to have permanent locations. The group tables can easily become designated work areas for portable centres that are in a tub. Teachers hang centre graphic and title signs above the tables as a simple way to identify these temporary centre homes.

(9) Display visual materials appropriate to the learning area.

Over the math manipulatives shelves, we placed number lines and math-related visuals and posters. Over the correspondence centre, we put large samples of letters. We put up several letters from a variety of authors. We placed several posters related to the writing process, the mechanics of writing and other grammar-related material on the walls near the writing centre. As you and the children develop material together, whether it is related to the theme or process you are working on, you will want to add to the visual material being displayed.

(10) Designate wall space in and near the classroom for children to display their work.

Our students have an art gallery area in the hallway outside the classroom where they can display their artwork. They also have wall space just outside the class where their posters are displayed, and a "Writer's Wall" is set up for displaying their writing. (See Chapter 8: Classroom Management and Organization.)

"A place for everything and everything in its labelled place" is an old adage adapted to a dynamic classroom. If all this is in place before the students arrive, you will be set for a smooth start up.

·········

Setting up the physical environment is just the beginning of the teacher's job. The next job is to prepare the planning board based on the centres you have decided to use. Each component of the dynamic classroom is so interconnected that you may often pull ahead on the chronology of our suggested order and then find you have to return to an earlier section of another component. That fits well with the analogy of an elastic holding all the parts together. Each time you work on one thing another will be affected.

The environmental set-up is influential in determining the atmosphere and events in the class as well as the type of learning and development of the student. Developing the class setting is an essential first step if educators want to pay more than lip service to the ideas of active, self-determined learners which are promoted by current theory and research. The learners in such an environment are extremely happy, motivated, self-sufficient explorers of their world, who continue to amaze us with the depth of research and learning that occur on a topic when given time, space, and opportunity to delve into it. This type of learning is certainly shaped by the environment.

Now that you have chosen the centres and created a learning space to provide for these centres you need to have a system in place that will allow the students to access the centres with ease. It is critical to put into place a system that gives some underlying control to the students but does not cause pandemonium. The following chapter will provide you with a how-to guide to construct, utilize, and maintain such a system.

CHAPTER **6**

MAKING AND USING THE CHECK-IN SYSTEM

The vitality of thought is in adventure. Ideas won't keep.
Something must be done about them.
— ALFRED NORTH WHITEHEAD

Once you have chosen the centres you will be using and you have created the environment to accommodate those centres, you are ready to start working on the details needed to keep your classroom functioning smoothly and efficiently. The structure which keeps the activity learning centre time organized is the check-in system.

What is a check-in system?

The check-in system has been adapted from the planning board found in *LOOK! HEAR!* published by Curriculum and Staff Development Services, The Board of Education for the City of North York, Ontario, in 1983. Originally promoted as a management system for teachers and students of kindergarten and early primary grades, we have adapted the system, and greatly enlarged the depth and variety of centres it accommodates. We have found this system works well up into the upper elementary grades. We have assisted teachers who wished to put it in place in classes up to grade six. Essentially, the check-in system serves to promote decision-making, accountability, negotiation, problem-solving, and responsibility without the student being dependent on the teacher.   Once it is up and running, the students use it without assistance from the teacher and it helps keep our whole activity time running smoothly.

The check-in system has two distinct parts — **The Centre Tickets** and **The Name Cards**. Each part is constructed with heavy bristol board large enough to hold the required number of self-adhesive library book pockets, as is shown on the following page.

The Centre Tickets have a pocket for each centre you plan on running for the year. We also have two pockets for "catch-up" with a set of six tickets in each pocket, and one pocket for the school library passes. The use of the library pass pocket is explained in Chapter 8: Classroom Management and Organization. As for the catch-up pocket it is explained in Chapter 13:

Up and Running. On each pocket is glued the representative graphic for each centre. We have found standard library book pockets are quite functional. In the pocket are the "tickets", also with the centre graphic on each. The number of tickets represent the maximum number of students you wish to have at each particular centre. This number may change ove the year and is easily managed by the addition or removal of the number of tickets.

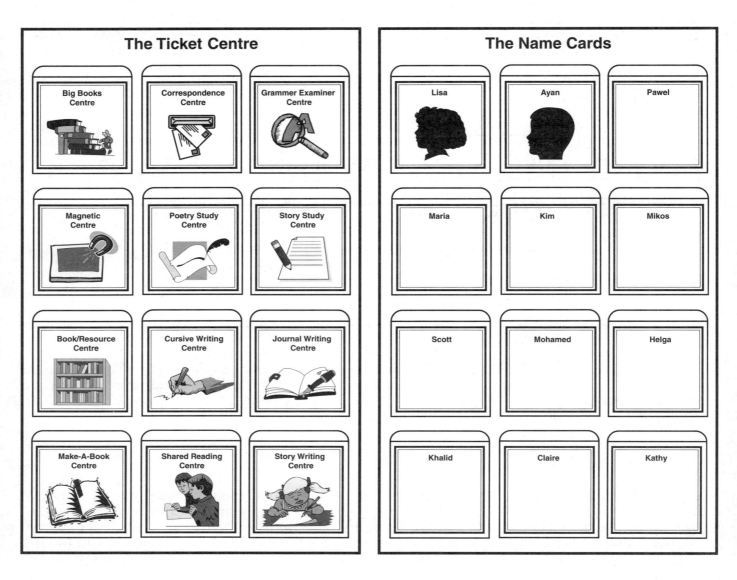

The Name Cards have a library pocket for each student with the student's name on each and one card in the pocket. Photos add a nice touch, to match the card to the pocket but if this is not possible, placing matching stickers on the card and pocket for each student, also adds a nice decorative touch. This also aids emergent readers and ESL students in finding their matching pocket when print dicrimination is difficult.

How it functions

The tickets act as the entry permits for each centre. When a student is required or wishes to participate at a centre, he takes a ticket from the centre pocket and places it in his name pocket, and puts his name card in the centre pocket. At a glance at the name cards one can see which students are at what centres. Likewise, when looking at the centre tickets board one can see which group of students is at one centre. This requires students to make a commitment and follow through with their choices.

Centres can be closed simply by removing all tickets for that centre and putting them in a safe place. You may wish to put in a stop sign or closed sign to reinforce it, but we have never found that to be necessary once the students learned how the system functions. A student who wishes to go to a centre that is occupied, looks at the centre board to see which of her friends are there. She then negotiates a time limit or trade. As the teacher, you are rarely bombarded with whining voices asking to go to a centre when the regulating system is clearly defined. It is hard to argue with the obvious: no ticket = no centre. This is perhaps one of the greatest benefits to the system.

The name cards can also serve as a system for checking attendance. When students arrive in the morning, they remove their card to a box or turn it face down (if you start the morning with a meeting) or they place it right away in the centre pocket where they are going. Cards that remain face up in the name pockets belong to those students who are absent. If the cards are placed in a box, when the centre time begins, the teacher can hand out each ticket to a student to make his/her centre choice thereby regulating the number of students rushing to get to the centre tickets.

Another useful purpose for the name pockets is to locate book borrowing slips. (See Chapter 8: Classroom Management and Organization.) When books are borrowed from the class book/resource centre, the students are required to fill out a book borrowing slip which can then be placed in their name pocket. When the book is returned the slip is removed. The teacher can easily identify which books still remain outstanding and who has them.

Variations

There are variations as to how this ticket system may operate. It is not absolutely necessary to have the name tickets, because students can just put the centre ticket in their name pocket and still have access to a centre. Also some teachers may have students choose their centre tickets for the week and work through them as the week progresses thereby managing their own time within the week time frame. Another variation is having no centre tickets but use only the name tickets to be placed in the centre pockets. To limit the number of participants, a number on the centre pocket could designate the limit.

No matter the format you wish to use for this system, you will find it invaluable in keeping things organized and flowing. Be warned that the students' daily reliable use of the check-in system does not happen overnight. You will have to have patience and consistency with your expectations. It may seem like it is never to going to run smoothly in the first few weeks but then it suddenly seems to come together.

The construction

Both the centre ticket board and the name card board are constructed using heavy bristol board. Using different colours for each board is helpful for quick discrimination. Library card pockets which are self-adhesive are used as the pockets. The school librarian is the best resource for ordering those. Before affixing the pockets to the bristol board, photocopy the graphics for each centre (see Blackline Masters #1-6) and also decide which identification symbols you will be using for the name cards. Then prepare the number of pockets. Lay out the pockets for each board to determine the spacing needed. Laminate both boards to reduce damage from wear and tear. Pockets can be carefully slit open using a sharp utility knife.

Choose a different colour of heavy card stock for the centre tickets and another colour for the name cards. We use red for the centre tickets, blue for the name tickets and pink for the catch-up tickets. Cut the tickets and cards to approximately 5 cm. x 15 cm. You should have at least eight tickets per centre and one name card per student. It is always a good idea to cut a few extra name cards to replace "lost cards" or for students admitted later in the year. Reduce the size of the centre graphics using a photocopier and make multiple copies. Once the graphics are on the tickets and cards, they too, should be laminated.

It is recommended that the centre ticket board and the name card board be mounted side by side in a convenient location at an accessible height for the students using them. When wall space was scarce, we used a chart stand and mounted the boards on opposite sides. Whatever the situation, it is important to keep in mind that the check-in system will be used daily and needs to operate smoothly and efficiently.

The students are quite happy to comply with the check-in system as it helps them keep organized. When they come in first in the morning, they go to the front board where they can see the "must-do" centre which again is clearly indicated using the same centre logo as is used on the centre pockets and the centre tickets. For example, a child in the pink parallelogram group goes to the front board, finds her group symbol, and will find the symbol for the required centre of the day posted neatly under it. Then the child has to go find the tub marked again with the same symbol and brings the tub which holds all the work materials for that centre to their group table. They then record in a work log their required centre activity for that day and get to work. (Further explanation of the work log is provided in Chapter 8: Classroom Management and Organization, and in Chapter 9: Evaluation and Authentic Assessment.)

....

Before centres can be made available to students, the materials for the activities have to be ready and waiting. Let's discuss specifically what these centres would have in them so that you are not stressed by the frequent demands of preparing activities all year long.

CHAPTER 7

THE LEARNING CENTRES

For the things we have to learn
before we can do them,
we learn by doing them.
—ARISTOTLE

What defines a learning centre?

You may have come across many different definitions of a learning centre over the years as the term has been widely used for close to twenty years now. Our definition, based on the extensive study of theorists and researchers, is as follows:

A learning centre is an activity or set of activities which attempt to produce a desired learning expectation or expectations. It needs to incorporate a degree of choice for the learner, allow for some differentiation of learning needs, connect to previous learning experiences and processes, reinforce and practice a set of skills, and not least of all, provide success for each learner.

What is a learning expectation or outcome?

Over the years, learning expectations and learning outcomes have been used interchangeably. Educational jurisdictions have curriculum documents regarding specific educational outcomes or expectations. The Ontario Ministry of Education and Training published a set of curriculum documents in 1994 entitled: *The Common Curriculum: Policies and Outcomes, Grades 1-9*. It outlined numerous specific learning outcomes in the core areas of curriculum. All of the specific learning outcomes stem from a set of basic expectations which drives all curriculum. The following ten essential learning outcomes were listed as the foundation of all learning. Our aim is to achieve these essential outcomes, so we have included them here to help clarify our overall aim of all centres.

1. Communicate effectively.
2. Solve problems and make responsible decisions using critical and creative thinking.
3. Use technology effectively.
4. Demonstrate an understanding of the world as a set of related systems.
5. Apply the skills needed to work and get along with other people.
6. Participate as responsible citizens in the life of the local, national and global communities.
7. Explore educational and career opportunities.
8. Apply aesthetic judgment in everyday life.
9. Make wise and safe choices for healthy living.
10. Use the skills of learning to learn more effectively.

All centres are set up with particular outcomes in mind. We expect children to have an opportunity to develop certain skills, values and knowledge during their time at any given centre. Each time we plan activities for a particular centre, we identify the particular outcome or outcomes which the students should attain at that centre. Defining outcomes or goals for each centre serves an integral role in how we develop the materials and guidelines for each particular centre. The goals for the centres described below are therefore clearly stated.

We cannot, however, list all the outcomes germane to each centre as there are so many outcomes that can be achieved at each centre. There are also so many crossovers and connections between the possible skills, values and knowledge gained at the centres that we merely focus on the goals that tend to identify why we use a particular centre. Our goals listed for the centres are not absolute but can be helpful to teachers planning centres in outcomes-based education.

Included in our bibliography is a list of resources which we have found helpful in understanding about learning. By understanding how children learn and the processes involved, we became much better at creating appropriate materials for centres which target certain outcomes.

Centres according to curriculum areas

Activities are planned, written and produced using desktop publishing for a possible sixty permanent activity centres. The centres we choose for the year vary from year to year and are dependent upon our assessment of the needs of a particular group of children. The selected group of centres for the year are available year-round but the material progresses through different skills and learning processes as the students develop. We have loosely organized the centres into six strands: language, math, science, technology/multimedia, the arts, and self and society. We say "loosely" because many centres can fit into other strands as well. The crossover from one strand to another is preferred as the hope of using such a model is that the curriculum be integrated. They consist of:

Language

big books centre	book/resource centre	chalkboard
correspondence centre	cursive writing centre	flannel board
grammar examiner centre	journal writing centre	spelling centre
magnetic board	make-a-book centre	novel study centre
poetry study centre	shared reading centre	
story study centre	story writing centre	

Math

banking/money centre	board games centre	calculator centre
calendar centre	consumer affairs centre	math blocks centre
math games centre	math problems centre	measurement centre
puzzles centre	sand table	

Science
  animal research centre   ecology centre   experiment centre
  inventions centre   research projects centre   science centre
  water table   weather centre

Technology/Multimedia
  audio centre   computer centre   construction centre
  design-a-solution centre   film projector centre   newspaper centre
  overhead projector centre   poster projects centre
  publishing centre   tape recording centre
  technology tools centre   video centre

The Arts
  art centre   dance centre   drama centre
  drawing centre   music centre   paint easel centre
  sculpture centre   toys centre

Self and Society
  Canadiana centre   cooking centre   history centre
  personal well being centre   map and globe centre

Materials and rationale for centres

Once we established the criteria for creating effective learning centres, we became much more adept at spotting useful materials and resources for outfitting the centres. In general we have found that good information sources, such as non-fiction books, and a wide variety of good books are essential. Keep your eye out also for good old-fashioned materials, like wooden blocks, board games, die, game counters, cards, flash cards, science equipment - thermometers, tubing, cylinders, measuring cups, and magnifying glass for instance. Make yourself a list and keep it handy because you will never know when you might hit a good garage sale, be at the dollar store, or come across some unique sidewalk sale. As much as possible we will list the types of things we have found useful over the years to have for each centre we have created.

This is our complete list of learning centres, in alphabetical order for each strand, with a small description, rationale, and suggested materials. It is not intended that you create each one of these centres nor that you choose exclusively from one strand. As mentioned in Chapter 4, you will need to make choices. It is recommended that you choose from each strand so as to create an integrated curriculum. We have grouped all possible centres into strands so that you can also see what centres could be joined together for easier management.

While this centre list is not exhaustive, these centres can provide classroom teachers with a selection that will serve them and their students for years. Our learning centres have been built around:

1. identification of a required open-ended or specific task,
2. involvement in some learning activity,
3. recording/reporting of the activity, and
4. reflecting on the learning that has occurred.

Most often the centre tasks are open-ended wherever possible. This allows for a greater degree of differentiation to occur relative to the abilities of the students attempting the task. It also benefits the teacher by freeing her up to attend to other teaching demands. Such centre tasks are usable for a long period of time and can be revisited throughout the year. When tasks are too specific they can usually only be used once and often require prerequisite skills.

Read through this extensive list and then hone in on the ones that will suit your classroom needs. As you read our centre descriptions you will inevitably think of a modification, improvement, or addition.

Language-related centres

The Big Books Centre has evolved into two functions. Children can read, share and respond to commercially published big books. Big books work wonderfully for shared reading by a large group. At reading time, small groups of students can cluster around a single big book. Once big books are used in the classroom, students become interested in co-operatively designing their own class big book. In such a book, for younger students, a particular frame or phrase is incorporated into each page after a particular topic or unit or special event has occurred. Older students need only a topic area or suggested overall design to begin a big book. Each student has the responsibility of designing one large page for the class big books. We try to have big books which cover a number of genres like poetry, riddles, science facts, math problems and art. The class big book is a good demonstration of what has been learned.

The purpose of this centre is to encourage students to retell/read aloud texts with confidence. When producing a class big book, they will be incorporating the strategies of the writing process using their own experience and information sources to record ideas, revise, and edit. They will also experience collaboration in working to produce a product shared by everyone.

The rough draft portion of the student's big book page is usually completed at a topic related centre such as the writing centre, poetry centre, art centre, science centre, or correspondence centre. The final good copy is completed here at the Big Book Centre for inclusion in the published book. Our class recently published a big book entitled, *Out of This World Postcards* concluding a study of the solar system. At the art centre, art work picturing one planet was done using pastels and black paint wash. At the correspondence centre, students wrote postcards, using the writing process, from and about their chosen planet. Then at this centre they put their final copies of their postcards and paintings together on a page to make the big book.

What you will need:
- a selection of trade big books
- response questions
- blank pages with frames for class big book
- interesting big book formats
- writing materials

The Book and Resource Centre is the library corner in our class. It houses a large variety of good quality fiction and nonfiction books. We try to provide a variety in the types of literature and in the range of works. These include stories, picture books, poetry, novels, diary accounts, historical fiction, science and technology-based information books, big books, atlases, dictionaries, map books, word books, encyclopedias and so on. The students' own published works are kept there as well to validate and provide models for other readers/writers in the class.

As much as possible books are categorized for the students, and are accessible to them. There are a few special books we keep out of reach of children, but they are made aware they exist and can make a request to use them. Because budgets don't allow for instant building of such a centre, we have often gone to alternate sources for books. Garage sales and book fairs, used book banks, and donations by parents have often provided us with good children's books. We are also permitted to do long-term borrowing from our school library which we can then house in our classroom. This has been particularly helpful when we are covering a particular topic or theme and it allows us to temporarily broaden the available selections on that area of interest.

When this centre is on the must-do list for the week, children are required to examine the features of books in progressive detail, respond to books, and use books for data collection. Children become familiar with terms such as author, publisher, editor, ISBN, copyright, and dedication. They are then better at getting information when it is needed. The goal of this centre is to become familiar with the features of published and bound material as well as story content. Students are encouraged to read a variety of text materials independently. They deal with different aspects of a book such as the table of contents, index, and key visuals. They have the opportunity to explore the differences between fiction and non-fiction books as well as compare them to magazines.

What you will need:
- as many quality books as you can get
- response sheets, cards, questions
- data collection sheets
- magazine boxes
- bins, baskets
- accessible shelving placed to create a reading corner
- cushions or comfortable seating
- a coding system to keep books categorized

The Chalkboard Centre encourages younger children especially to take their first steps at writing. You can set aside a small space of the large classroom chalkboard for centre use or use small slate style boards that are available commercially. Chalkboards are also useful for practising computations, printing and cursive writing. Children find the fluidity of using large motor muscles a little easier to get the letter/number formation when they are first starting out. Students also like to work out story lines by drawing and retelling their stories to a partner. Whatever the end result, the chalkboard is another medium which encourages children to practice necessary skills in handwriting, literacy or numeracy.

What you will need:
- a designated chalkboard space or
- at least 6 individual slate boards
- variety of coloured chalk
- chalk brushes or thick socks to act as "chalk mitts"

The Correspondence Centre provides students with the opportunities to learn the conventions of letter writing, postcards, memos, and messages. As much as possible students write real correspondence and send it or mail it to a real recipient. Authors such as Robert Munsch, John Bianchi, and Phoebe Gilman have been recent respondents. There is much excitement when the student receives a letter in response! Students also like to write to former students or teachers and are always eager to get a reply. Others have written to companies or associations for freebies or information. On occasion, students have written mock letters, when taking on an imaginary role for the purpose of stretching their imagination and exploring ideas. Most recently, students have taken to using the Internet as a vehicle for sending greeting cards and postcards via e-mail. We have also produced a living letter on video which we've sent to a school in Virginia. Whatever the medium, students value communicating and corresponding with another.

What you will need:
- a variety of stationary, notepaper, message paper, envelopes
- addresses on index cards in a file box
- guidelines for writing a friendly letter, a business letter, postcards, memos and addressing envelopes
- situations for writing

The Cursive Writing/Printing Centre allows children to practise their skills in producing neat and legible writing. Children want to explore the transition between printing and cursive and need opportunities to look at different ways of forming written letters. At this centre, children follow handwriting guide books to form letters in practice books. Eventually, their own style of handwriting emerges. We usually have the youngest children begin with the letters of the alphabet and their own name. Older children use practice cards or text from books.

What you will need:
- letter formation charts
- writing practise cards
- writing practise notebooks

The Flannel Board   When we taught children in the earlier grades we enjoyed using flannel boards. They are a great visual tool for promoting language development and story telling and retelling. Such literacy events are often the jumping-off point for story writing for younger children who still respond to visual effects. At the flannel board centre children either make up a story using the flannel people, creatures or objects, or they retell an already told tale. Being able to move these small flannel representational characters and props is a joy to children who want or realize a need for changes. Once children are satisfied with the sequence of the story, they write it in strips and put them on the board, or write their own little book on the story. Parent volunteers can be helpful in designing and cutting out new flannel characters. Commercially produced flannel materials are still readily available and can also be used for demonstrating math concepts, sorting, ordering, and categorizing in science.

What you will need:
- flannel board
- flannel characters and props from stories
- flannel numbers, letters, shapes, and figures
- task cards
- variety of response possibilities: small blank booklets, sheets of regular sized paper divided into 4, 6, or 8 boxes, in which children can draw the story

The Grammar Examiner Centre is where children explore the parts of speech and the rules of language. They read examples and samples and then either write their own examples illustrating a particular rule of language or give a correct usage where they unearth the "rule". We expected that children would find this centre rather tedious and boring but most children are pleased to come to a rather straight-forward centre.

What you will need:
- task cards
- student books regarding the rules of language

Journal Writing has been incorporated into the language curriculum of many classrooms over the past decade. There are many different ways that teachers and students use journal writing; however, it is understood that this type of writing tends to involve reflective, personal accounts of the writers' experiences. Teachers may respond to the ideas presented but as this is a personal piece of work, they may not offer any suggestions regarding the mechanics of writing. Students can then focus on writing about what they want to say as opposed to how they have to punctuate the sentence or spell a word. Personal writing is a draft copy of writing and not meant to be taken through further steps in the process of writing.

   We use the journal centre as an opportunity for students to reflect on their learning in our classroom, set personal goals, or to share personal anecdotes, achievements, and ideas. Students are encouraged to express themselves through drawing in their journal as well. We sometimes lead that process by leaving at the centre particular questions about their learning, or about their handling of social situations. These topics or questions go from the specific to the general. Some examples are: What observations and conclusions can you make about the art work demonstrated by our visitor from the art gallery? What has been your favourite activity during the past week (month, term, cycle, year), and explain why? Why do you think the visiting author chose to write about the topic of her book? How might you handle the situation of getting to know a new student, and so on. Journal writing allows the teacher an insight into what works and what doesn't work well in the class; it can show personal preferences, and give teachers another assessment tool for their programme.

What you will need:
- notebooks for each student (learning logs)
- suggestions for personal reflection, and prompts

The Magnetic Centre is geared toward younger students. Access to a magnetic surface provides children with the chance to manipulate magnetic letters, numbers and shapes. They may be asked to put together a message for their classmates, a word, phrase, or list, such as colours, or days of the week etc. With numbers they can do computation, or develop a number pattern. With shapes they can describe them, identify them, develop patterns. Combining the letters and patterns and numbers can provide challenging yet interesting tasks for the students.

What you will need:
- magnetic boards or use blackboard
- magnetic letters, numbers, shapes, etc.

The Make-a-Book Centre arose from the need of some children to write little books about the topics at hand. We discovered that by providing the scaffold of an already produced format it is not as scary as starting out writing on a blank page. Students enjoy either exploring a topic or revisiting the information they already know about something. We provide them with a book frame that is very open-ended. This allows them to personalize the project and it allows them to complete a booklet in just one sitting. For example, we often use the "I Like" book at the beginning of the year. Each page begins with "I like... because..." with plenty of room to add more. There is space both for text and for illustrations on each page. The books have a cover and author's page and are made available stapled and ready to complete. The students do not follow the full writing process here but are encouraged to check their own spelling and work to do their best. For the reluctant writer this is a way to achieve a measure of success and have a pleasing product. It also encourages younger children to take the plunge in writing their own books. These booklets are often chosen for the writers' wall selection as they can look polished relatively quickly and children can enjoy a sense of accomplishment about writing a book that doesn't take the same time as when they write their own stories from scratch.

What you will need:
- book frame booklets with a variety of styles and topics

The Novel Study Centre As children's reading abilities progress, they sometimes need a little push to step up to a more challenging book than a picture or easy-reading book. The novel study centre was designed to encourage children to read a variety of quality novels, for all the reasons that reading such good quality literature exist. Children become particularly proud of themselves after finishing a novel. Once they have read the novel they are required to respond in some fashion. A variety of responses are suggested though at times we encourage children to create their own ideas for a response. For the latter, they make a plan and then have it approved. Today, materials about novel studies are readily available for teachers. Some examples of the kinds of responses to a novel are: draw a comic strip that shows the key parts of the novel, write a letter to the author commenting on the novel, plan a trip for one of the characters, describe it and tell why you chose the events of that trip, make a diorama of a main scene, or act out a key part.

What you will need:
- a good collection of novels for the classroom
- a system for borrowing those novels
- task cards

The Poetry Study Centre Children at the poetry centre enjoy, analyze, or create their own poems. We want children to explore the rhythm and rhyme of the lyrics of language. We are constantly amazed at the beautiful poems children write, their depth of expression, and their refinement of thought. Sometimes we have children create poetry around a theme. Sometimes just an area or category of topics is suggested, such as weather. Then these poems are written onto a template on the computer, printed, illustrated and collected and bound into a class book. Students can then borrow these books for sharing together or reading together during reading time. Occasionally we have children respond to a reading of a poem. Sometimes they like to draw some pictures in their sketch books to go with the poem after we read it to them.

What you will need:
- · a collection of poetry
- · a rhyming dictionary
- · task cards

The Shared Reading Centre Children love to read together in groups of two or more. They enjoy the story together and become more confident readers as they read with and to each other. Reading partners often select a book the other partner would not, thereby broadening the horizons of the children. New authors, new genres, new vocabulary and ideas are presented to the readers. Children who have shared a book treasure their time together and feel a kinship that otherwise would not have been created.

What you will need:
- · a variety of stories with multiple copies
- · selection of big books
- · response form or peer-reading conference form

The Spelling Centre provides students with the opportunity to explore new words, practise forming new words, and to see how words are connected. The children do this in a variety of ways, like finding and building words from a particular word 'family'; exploring, playing, and inventing word games; doing word puzzles and crosswords; finding the patterns in spellings to recognize spelling rules; using dictionaries to develop dictionary skills; and using a thesaurus or word processors.

What you will need:
- · spelling log books · task cards
- · word lists · word processors
- · word banks · thesaurus
- · word books
- · dictionaries

The Story Study Centre Our class day offers many opportunities for the reading and sharing of stories. Authors choose features, elements, and characteristics when writing a story. Students need to reflect on these components in order to understand various authors' choices when writing in certain genres. Because children are authors themselves they are very keen to understand why certain authors' works have certain characteristics. Children wish to respond to stories in many ways. Keeping in mind how we provide opportunities to strengthen all of the intelligences, we allow children to respond to stories in a wide variety of ways.

What you will need:
- · story study synopsis
- · story study web
- · story study question cards
- · variety of good children's literature

The Story Writing Centre is set up for children to write stories. We read stories every day so children are provided with examples of good children's literature. We allow students the freedom to choose the topic of their stories except for violent content. Children need to know they have the freedom to take their stories where they want in their imaginations. Children are encouraged to respond to each others' writing all along the writing process, causing the writer and the reader to reflect, revise, and refine their writing. The student's writing is clearly valued, and final published works are housed within our classroom library. Children may decide not to bring all works to a final copy stage.

What you will need:
- editing checklist
- blank rough draft writing booklets in different sizes
- writing process model
- writing response review sheet
- writing folders

Some suggestions for combining concepts/skills from the language-related centres are:

The Book/Resource Centre - to include Shared Reading.

The Writing Centre - to include Make-a-Book, Storywriting, Correspondence, Big Books.

The Word Study Centre - to include Grammar Examiner, Spelling.

The Genre Study Centre - to include Story Study, Novel Study, Poetry Study.

Math-related centres

The Banking/Money Centre is used to give students exposure to our currency, what it looks like, and the value of each denomination. At this centre students have explored the history and evolution of currency use and the significance of the visual symbols on each denomination. We have had children use the play money to go on a shopping spree and calculate what they could purchase. Younger children learn to identify the different coins by name as well as value. The banking/money centre can also deal with other forms of commerce such as cheques, bank accounts, credit cards and foreign currency.
    The purpose is to give children the opportunity to deal with money situations and to work on their math skills.

What you will need:
- tray with play money
- resources for the history of our money
- problem cards
- money stamps and ink pad

Board Games Centre allows students to participate in standard classic board games to reinforce their skills in math, spelling, reasoning, cooperative learning and the use of rules. They are required to write a report which outlines the rules of the game, its objective and the resulting outcome of the chosen game. We have purchased a lot of our board games at garage sales or resurrected them from our homes once our own children had outgrown them.

What you will need:
- a variety of commercially produced board games
- a report form
- we recommend the following games:
  Scrabble, Monopoly, Sorry, Tic Tac Toe, Pictionary, Snakes & Ladders,
  Battleship, Mastermind, Touché, Boggle, Clue, Checkers, Chess

The Calculator Centre is used to give students the opportunity to work with the calculator to solve problems. The tasks begin with understanding the different features of the calculator and what each part is used for. Then tasks progress in difficulty, working through the different functions of arithmetic. There are many commercially produced task cards available ready to use and are supported with a report or recording reproducible page. There is also an overhead calculator available which allows the calculator's whole image to be projected for the whole class to see or if being used by a small group.

What you will need:
- student calculators
- overhead calculator
- task cards
- report form

The Calendar Centre was created to reinforce the skills of using a calendar, understanding the sequence and accumulation of days, weeks, months, years, and centuries and being able to make calculations based on the calendar. As so much of our lives is regulated by the calendar, this centre tries to present situations and questions which help students become more familiar with its use. The goals are to reinforce math skills and also to become familiar with holidays, festivals, and events celebrated by different cultures.

What you will need:
- as many quality different forms of calendars you can find from the current year and past years such as daily calendars, monthly formats, and whole years at a glance.
- task cards
- information books related to holidays and festivals
- blank calendar forms
- recording sheets
- flash cards of the days, and months to sort and order

The Consumer Affairs Centre was created to give students the opportunity to understand the different types of markets we are faced with as consumers; the meaning of wholesale, on sale, final sale, guarantee, for rent, and promotion; and what consumers need to be aware of when making purchases. It is an area of authentic learning and will benefit students for years as they build on their knowledge and experiment with the related terminology and concepts through problem-solving and role playing.

What you will need:
- catalogues, newspaper ads, want-ads, *Renters News, Auto Trader, Penny Saver*, etc.
- task cards

The Math Blocks Centre allows children to identify, extend and create patterns with a variety of math blocks and use these patterns to build models, and solve problems. Students can investigate two and three-dimensional figures by constructing models of them. They are sometimes asked to describe the results of sliding, flipping, and turning objects and shapes, using their knowledge of spatial relationships. Children use a variety of shapes and solids including pattern blocks, attribute blocks, centicubes. They enjoy using overhead blocks on the overhead projector especially when they are building a tiling pattern or a quilt pattern from the pattern blocks. There are a variety of commercially produced task cards for solving problems or puzzles using pattern blocks and tangrams. Students are required to reflect on what they have chosen and completed, and record their activity in a report with a diagram.

What you will need:
- variety of math manipulatives or blocks such as pattern blocks, unifix cubes, attribute blocks, tan grams, multi-link, etc.

- blocks for the overhead projector
- tracing templates for pattern blocks, shapes, attribute blocks, tangrams
- geometric solids
- task cards
- report forms

The Math Games Centre makes the repetitive nature of learning basic math skills fun. As children are tossing two bean bags on a number grid, and recording results of a designated operation they are learning their addition and multiplication facts. Here the children can be investigating the nature of fractions and decimals through a game. Many math programs provide games which can be copied and laminated and kept together in Ziploc® bags. You will need to collect a variety of dice and counters, as well.

What you will need:
- a number of of math games
- timer
- counters and die
- task cards
- report forms

The Math Problems Centre is where children solve a variety of math problems and select appropriate calculation methods. For those who still need them, manipulatives are made available. At this centre students estimate, calculate, and/or check solutions on a calculator. Children are given problems to practise skills and to extend their thinking about practical applications to problems.

What you will need:
- math task cards
- math notebooks

The Measurement Centre Children need lots of real experience with concepts such as distance, time and weight to come to understand what measurement is. Here children estimate, measure and/or calculate, and record temperature, time, length, perimeter, area, capacity, volume, distance, and speed using appropriate units of measurement. They use both standard and non-standard units of measure. Children measure and compare themselves, their classroom, their school and relate sizes of large animals to numbers of children and so on. They use measuring tapes, metric sticks, rulers, balances, weights, scales, clocks, graduated cylinders, and stop watches. As children become more experienced with weights and measures they become better at being able to estimate and being able to relate one thing to another.

What you will need:
- a variety of measuring tools: weights, scales, measuring tapes, metric, and yard sticks, graduated cylinders, litre buckets, stopwatch, thermometers
- task cards   • report forms

The Puzzle Centre is provided for students who enjoy and need to practise visual and spatial challenges. Sorting, grouping and problem solving are some of the skills used in doing puzzles. Puzzles also are a great source of information, especially ones that have been designed for educational purposes. Many commercially-produced puzzles provide educational accompanying legends. Puzzle building also provides wonderful opportunities for cooperative work. We particularly like to put this centre out early in the year to get children working together with the new children in the classroom. Watching children work on puzzles provides the teacher with lots of clues about the different ways a child approaches problem solving. Some systematically sort pieces by colour, shape, size, etc. Others do a lot of studying of the picture first before they begin. What is even more interesting is to listen to them as they build the puzzle and see how their thinking unfolds. There are more sophisticated puzzles available that move beyond the standard jigsaw puzzle as well. We also have available a report form which asks children to reflect on the strategies they use to build or solve a puzzle, how long it takes them, and what they liked about it.

What you will need:
- jigsaw puzzles
- floor puzzles
- wooden puzzles
- math puzzles
- boards or plexiglass as mobile work surfaces for the puzzles
- report forms

The Sand Centre should be standard equipment in primary classrooms. It allows children to fill up and empty containers, and so come to understand density, mass, and measurement, while having a great tactile experience. Students can become involved in imaginative play where they take on and assign roles. This can be a great place for language development. By strategically placing certain equipment teachers can orchestrate the kinds of activities they want to see there. For example, a teacher may want children to experiment filling up different sizes of containers and measuring their weight with both non-standard and standard units of measurement. They can then ask the children to record their findings on a chart. Then they can make comparisons in a report. For example, the report might indicate which one is heaviest, lightest, the same, heavier than the lightest and so on. In this way children become adept later on in estimating size and weight.

What you will need:
- sand table
- task cards
- materials for children to use, like plastic shovels, a variety of containers, dump trucks, weights, etc.
- report forms

When starting out you may wish to have one generic **Math Centre** where children can do all math tasks, such as use blocks, play games, practice problems, work on a calculator, and encounter measurement. You would just change the task cards in order to change your specific focus. It is easier to take this route during your first year as you sort things out.

Science-related centres

The Animal Research Centre is built for children to study the world of animals. At this centre we often begin with classification and categorizations. It is a means of getting children to understand different characteristics of animals and their relationship to the environment. This centre also provides the opportunity to do independent research projects on an animal of choice in the form of small and large projects. Inquiry learning, research, and project writing processes drive this centre. We have found that children engaged in learning about animals gain tremendous knowledge about the physical world. They not only learn about the animal, but also about related geographical, environmental, and ecological concerns and how these are connected to their local and global community. They learn about scientific phenomena such as adaptation, camouflage, and life cycles. Students compare and contrast basic characteristics of living things; investigate the features of animals that help them to survive their habitat; explore the basic needs of living things; compare and contrast the characteristics of individuals of the same species; and understand the terms adaptation, survival, endangered, and extinct in relation to animal species and biomes.

What you will need:
- non-fiction animal resources
- library request forms
- research outline booklet
- rough draft folder with recording strips
- model of the animal research steps
- animal research checklist
- final copy booklets

The Ecology Centre The focus of the ecology centre is to study the interrelationships of animals, plants, and the environment. Children need to understand the value of respecting the environment and look for ways to make a positive contribution. At this centre you can evolve the focus from simply looking at the particular characteristics of plants and animals to the characteristics of different ecological biomes to the environmental issues and crises around the world. We have had children explore solutions to problems, create new habitats for animals, design a new animal for a given habitat, and research different uses for natural resources.

What you will need:
- non-fiction resources available on various aspects of the environment, plants, animals
- task cards
- recording, reporting, creating, designing materials that match the required tasks

The Experiment Centre allows children to do experiments through which they will come to know the features and properties of matter and forces in their world. At the centre students are given a choice of a few experiments that are usually on a related topic and are related to the current environmental study focus. For example, when studying weather, children made clouds, explored the effects of cold and warm air on air pressure and so on. Such activities are usually done in a group where all children work together or in clusters of two or three to do the experiment. Then they each write out an individual report. The forms we have designed accommodate the variety of abilities in the groups. We usually put all the materials needed for the experiments in the activity centre bins, for ease of set-up. However, if needed, we set up materials ahead of time and designate a spot for that centre.

What you will need:
- variety of science-related equipment such as: graduated cylinders, thermometers, balloons, straws, stopwatch, variety of tools, weights and measures, bottles, rubber hoses, magnifying glasses, magnets, pulleys, etc.
- task cards
- report forms

The Inventions Centre is a great deal of fun. At this centre children not only get to read about how things were invented, who invented them and some obstacles that people overcame, but they can invent their own machine, or object. This centre can incorporate many facets of the study of inventions, having an historical purpose, a scientific or technological focus or one which allows the student to try out her/his ideas. Children are required to submit a written plan before they build their invention. Once it is approved children have frequently given long hours of attention to the project. We like children to reflect on the process once the project is complete, so that they self evaluate the effectiveness of its use, the materials used, how things were joined, and so on. Their report must also include a diagram, description, evaluation and ideas for improvement should anyone else like to try making their own inventions.

What you will need:
- books on inventions   • report form   • task cards
- materials for building inventions (e.g., tubes, wheels, gears, elastic, straws, wooden sticks, boxes, and wire, etc.)

The Science Centre promotes curiosity, investigation, exploration, creativity and problem solving that helps form a student's understanding of the world as a whole, the interrelationship of the environment and people. It promotes risk-taking, and systematic, objective investigations. Task cards at the centre usually ask the scientist to select certain materials, do an investigation, solve the problem or respond to the challenge. After observing the results of the subsequent activity, students record findings, relate that information to previous knowledge and draw conclusions. The student scientists can make recommendations, and/or issue further challenges, based on the results of their own work. A report form is submitted and shared with peers.

What you will need:
- tools to observe, measure, calculate, represent, create, identify and describe, examples: thermometers, pulleys and other simple machines, microscopes, magnifying glasses, varied beakers and tumblers, rulers, etc.
- sample investigation cards
- sample baseline/knowledge sheets
- recording blank
- problem cards
- science notebooks
- task cards

The Research Projects Centre Without doubt one of the ways that our students prefer to learn is through investigating a topic through research projects. When children are given options they key into those things that interest them, thereby plugging into motivational factors. We teach children the research process in large group lessons. Then we introduce them to increasingly more difficult criteria for the research project. We usually introduce this centre after each child has successfully completed a project at the animal research centre. Children who are with us for more than one year often request to access this centre early in the year. They feel truly successful when they stand before the class and give a report on a topic about which they have become very knowledgeable. They become "experts" on that topic and we refer other students to them. We give children guidelines and criteria governing a particular project. For example, when students want to do a country research project, we give them a list of areas they should cover such as location, climate, vegetation, animals, currency used, religions, customs, flag, famous tourist attractions, famous people from that country, etc. For younger students we usually give them a simplified version of the list, and the information they research and write is put on a poster. As children advance in their abilities to read, synthesize and write this information, many prefer to write a full length report. We usually require that some illustrations accompany these projects. Of course, when children are comfortable with the research process they then can design their own project. They put so much more into their efforts when they have designed their project; we have had excellent projects presented to us. This is not only for older students either. We have a grade 2 student who has developed a research project about the desert because she wanted to know how animals survive in the desert. She refined the categories to include "Features of the desert", "Deserts of the world", "Desert climate", "Animals in the desert", and "Desert animals habits". She is learning the answer to her original question and much more.

What you will need:
- research report outline cards
- rough draft booklets
- research checklists
- variety of informational books in your classroom library
- blank report booklets for final copy

The Water Centre When used as a centre, a water table provides students with the opportunity for many math, science, and technology discoveries and activities. Children can investigate the properties of measurement and capacity. They investigate the materials and physics of floating/sinking, for example, by filling up containers, graduated cylinders, weighing, recording and comparing. They test their self-made water crafts, checking water-proof adhesions, materials, and designs. Students always record and report their findings. It is advisable to provide waterproof aprons, to prevent younger children from getting wet. When the water table is used as a centre, with strict guidelines and requirements, it has served us well as a wet laboratory.

What you will need:
- a water table
- measuring cups, graduated cylinders
- bottles
- rafts, floating devices
- task cards
- report forms

The Weather Centre The many variances in weather in Canada prove that this is one area of study about which we will all benefit from knowing. Floods, ice storms, tornadoes, and forest fires in our country have demonstrated the magnificent forces that contribute to our weather, and therefore our lives. Children examine the different types of clouds and their relation to the weather, the extremes of weather and their causes, the water cycle, the seasons, and the tools that are used to measure and predict weather. Students do experiments to learn about high and low pressure, for example, or they may examine the weather graph in the newspaper or create one of their own. Our students make graphs based on rainfall, temperature, cloud coverage, and the hours of daylight, to name a few.

What you will need:
- weather instruments: anemometer, barometer, thermometer, etc.
- a variety of informational books, posters, and pamphlets on weather
- task cards
- report forms

Some suggestions for combining concepts/skills from the science-related centres are:

The Science Centre - to include Inventions, Experiments.

The Ecology Centre - to include Weather.

The Research Centre - to include Animal Research.

The Water/Sand Centre - to include Sand and used interchangeably as needed.

Technology/Multimedia-related centres

The Audio Centre consists of a tape recorder or CD player with several headphones. Listening for information and enjoyment are encouraged. This centre is often referred to as a listening centre. At the audio centre, small groups of students or individuals can hear the recordings of stories or poems. Children can join in the reading with multiple copies of a book, respond to the reading in a variety of ways, and record their responses. The audio centre can also be used for non-fiction information. More publishers are making such resources available, and sometimes these books come with a film strip. At an audio centre, students have had to listen to music related to a theme/topic and have had to illustrate what they hear. They have had to identify sounds. For example, they had to identify different Canadian animal sounds which they then had to write about and draw the animal the sound represented.

The goals of this centre are for students to read while listening to a variety of texts and respond to them. They identify different types of texts and some of the characteristics. In their responses, they have the opportunity to express their thoughts and feelings, and explain the intended meaning of the texts, as well as formulate opinions.

What you will need:
- tape or CD player with attachments for up to six headphones
- a variety of recorded material with visual or book copies where appropriate
- response sheets, questions, and prompts

The Computer Centre requires that you designate one or more classroom computers to this centre during activity centre time. (We provide our students with weekly sessions in a computer lab beyond the classroom.) The purpose of this centre is to build a student's computer awareness and literacy. We encourage students to access information on the various CD Roms available such as the *World Book Encyclopedia, Groliers Encyclopedia, Information Finder*, atlas, and *The Way Things Work* or via the Internet. There are also storybooks which are interactive and encouraging for beginning readers and there are a number of high quality educational games available. These days the selections seem endless. Lists of recommended computer resources are available in computer magazines and education journals. (The goals at this centre do not include using the computer for producing materials, such as publishing stories, creating spreadsheets, or preparing a document. That is part of the **Publishing Centre** listed below.)

What you will need:
- a computer with CD Rom capability
- access to CD Roms of various genres
- a storage system for the easy care of the CD's
- Internet log book and approved address book

The Construction Centre focuses mainly on the use of building blocks for the creation of structures built by small groups of students. For building using hand tools and raw materials we have the Technology Centre. If you didn't want to have too many centres to begin with, it is possible to combine the two ideas and have the different building approaches available at different times at the one centre. We find it valuable to have the students reflect and report on the building process they use.

What you will need:
- blocks such as *LEGO, Construx* (by Fisher Price), *Googolplex, Mechano, Tinker Toy*
- a report form
- a short term display area is an added bonus

The Design-a-Solution Centre permits students to become architects and engineers. They are usually given a problem, and are asked to design a solution. For example a structure may be required to solve a problem in the area of ecology, or animal safety. Students may be involved in school or local projects such as designing better play areas in their school yards. Sometimes a structure is shown that has problems and students are asked to think of ways to redesign the item so that it functions better. Big Books that show "what's wrong with this picture" are useful. Some books come ready-made with specific problems that need to be solved using a set of specified criteria. You may also find books that have larger kinds of problems focussing on the environment such as traffic congestion, water shortages, or air pollution. You also can find your own problem situations by linking to literature. Find any known story "problems" and have children build models of a solution such as a very strong chair for Baby Bear. Students complete a report in which they must sketch out their plan/design, label the various components and describe all the steps in their solution, thereby practising procedural language. The sky is the limit for possibilities in task variety at this centre, because children can really let their imaginations run free, yet the solutions have to based on the laws of physics and science.

What you will need:
- a good variety of informational books related to the topic you wish to cover
- task cards
- report forms
- lots of recycled materials

The Filmstrip Projector Centre is where students watch filmstrips for a specific purpose. Some filmstrips have an accompanying audio tape to discuss the picture in each frame. Others have accompanying texts. The filmstrip projector is often seen as an outdated piece of equipment. However, we have found that there are great old filmstrips on a variety of topics ranging from grammar, stories, math, geology, and history. Even some science-related films are still very pertinent, for example, the parts of a flower, or the different types of clouds. Librarians in the past were glad to clean out their old filmstrips and give them to us. One of the things we enjoy about these old projectors is that the students themselves can operate them and they have control over how fast or slow they go. They can review as often as needed. One day we will probably discard this piece of equipment but right now it still is a valuable learning tool. Unlike trying to access the Internet on the classroom computers we are always sure we can access the filmstrips.

What you will need:
- filmstrip projector
- variety of filmstrips
- report forms

The Newspaper Centre Because our world is one where print is so prevalent, we want children to extract meaning from it in all its forms. Children come to know the power of print when they become involved in the writing of a newspaper or newsletter. Newspapers make up an important element of gathering information about the world we live in. Children can learn early on not only the sorts of news items available from their community but also from around the world. They can comparison shop through the advertisements, learn about the leaders in our world, look into the arts world, the sports, fashion, home, cooking, gardening and the like. They can write their own news stories, create their own comic strips, and write advertisements. Two key tasks at this centre are the analysis of the parts of a newspaper, and and the writing of parts of a paper. It is very simple to set up a template on the classroom computer, have children write their stories on a rough draft, conference with the teacher and then have groups of children put the parts together to publish their own paper. In such papers, they can write about what's happening at their school, publish interviews of visitors or write about environmental issues relevant to the community.

What you will need:
- a regular supply of newspapers, especially community and local papers
- task card
- computer and access to a printer

The Overhead Projector Centre We decided to have this as a centre when we noticed how much children loved using the overhead projector during our math classes. As we accumulated materials for this centre we realized that this could provide children with the opportunity to practice or explore many math skills or concepts. Then we realized that through the use of good overheads, children could examine any topic such as geography, poetry and science. Diagrams are easily seen and examined. In addition the overhead allows students opportunity to create, experiment or develop a variety of designs. Children are intrigued by the fact that the overhead projector exaggerates the size of the image. With colour overlays, they can experiment with colour. Depending on our purpose for its use, we provide different materials for the different needs.

What you will need:
- overhead projector
- a variety of overhead math materials, such as the acrylic, see-through materials that have been created for overhead use, available through educational catalogues. They include pattern blocks, small coloured discs, and squares, overhead calculator, and large selection of overheads transparencies on a variety of topics such as maps, diagrams, language analysis, parts of a letter, etc.
- task cards
- report forms

The Poster Projects Centre We designed this centre after noticing the many times children requested to make posters as a way of displaying the information they had gathered on a project or topic. We also realized that children gather lots of information from posters. Posters provide a mixed medium of print and picture or illustration. Students set up posters so that their components are balanced while still getting the information across to the viewer. Children who make posters use many skills, such as researching the topic, organizing the information, illustrating, and doing the layout. We not only ask students to create posters at this centre, but ask them to respond to posters created professionally and those made by classmates. We provide the students with the basic requirements for creating posters.

What you will need:
- poster guidelines
- good supply of poster paper
- variety of coloured pencils, poster paints, brushes, etc.
- collection of commercially made posters
- task cards

The Publishing Centre When we direct children to write, we bring them through the writing process of brainstorming, rough draft, rewriting, conferencing, rewriting, and final draft. We often give students options of how to present their final draft. Sometimes it is in the form of a hand-written project, though most often student writers want to see their final copy as polished looking as possible, and therefore choose to have their work published on the computer. We provide children with two different formats for publication. Firstly, children can access templates which we have put on their writing files on the computer so they simply type onto the template. The teacher checks this work before it is printed. Secondly, children can simply type their work just using script, without any formatting. We then help format their stories into paragraphs or by some other organizational unit and print them out. Next, the child glues the unit onto template pages we have created and photocopied. Then we merely photocopy the glued copy, giving us a fairly polished final product, which the child leaves in our class library. The glued copy can go home to be shared with family.

What you will need:
- computers with desktop publishing, or word processing software
- teacher-created blank book templates

The Tape Recording Centre Children not only need to listen to recordings, they should also have the opportunity to record things themselves. At this centre students do interviews and tape their own reading. We ask children to record mystery sounds, and write out clues in a quiz format. Children work through many tasks at this centre, developing skills and abilities in a broad range of areas, and then are able to reflect on their product by listening to and by sharing their recordings.

What you will need:
- a tape deck with microphone and taping capacity
- blank tapes   • report form

(This centre can be incorporated under the **Audio Centre** and the required task changed from listening to recording.)

The Technology Tools Centre The focus of the technology tools centre is the disassembling of machines, electronic and other equipment. Students examine materials and use tools like screwdrivers and wrenches. They may explore where and how technology is being used, evaluate the effect of technology on people and their environment, and the history of technology. They draw and label samples of the technology they are exploring. They can use piping to create a plumbing system or put together an electrical circuit using wire, a battery and a light bulb.

What you will need:
- castaway machinery such as radios, clocks, telephones, toasters
- tools
- wires, batteries, light bulbs
- screws, nuts and bolts, etc.
- report forms
- task cards

The Video Centre Our world is increasingly one of visual messages accompanied by sound bites. Children of today need to not only be able to take meaning from such a medium but to understand how it is created. We want our students to be comfortable with the medium, to explore the creative aspects of it while delivering a message. Children at this centre often respond to this centre by viewing and reacting to it, somewhat as a critic or reviewer. The children use the equipment themselves and learn how to scan and replay. For some, this is their only opportunity to become familiar with such technology. Children respond to the immediacy of the medium. It is very good for them to know when advertising, for example, is trying to manipulate them or use stereotypes. Children can also produce videos at this centre, if you have access to a video camera. They become adept at taking the shots, and writing and editing the accompanying text. Students love to see themselves on camera, and will work hard to create polished effects.

What you will need:
- video camera
- VCR with remote
- prerecorded tapes on various topics
- blank tapes
- task cards
- response forms

Suggested combinations for reducing the number of technology/multimedia centres are:

The Technology Centre - to include Design-a-Solution, Technology Tools, and Construction.

The Print Media Centre - to include Newspaper and Poster Projects. (This centre includes other forms of print such as magazines, advertisements, etc.)

The Multimedia Centre - to include Audio, Tape Recording, Film Projector, Overhead Projector, Video.

The Computer Centre - to include Publishing.

The Arts-related centres

The Art Centre is designed to allow children the opportunity to increase their knowledge of art techniques, media, art history, and to develop their own art-related skills, as well as to develop an appreciation for the art world. A variety of open-ended tasks, media, and opportunities are provided at this centre, as well as specific tasks which are created to help develop a student's own skills, knowledge and values involving the art world. Students are encouraged to reflect on and discuss design ideas, techniques and styles used in their own and others' works of art. They use art projects to explore current topics and issues and explore personal and cultural experiences as subject matter in their art work.

What you will need:
- variety of art supplies
- models of works of art
- a variety of books related to art history

The Dance Centre provides children with the opportunity to respond to music through movement. They explore rhythm and the many ways of responding to it. Dance for students is usually covered in books for physical education programs. You can design your tasks in a variety of ways, going from free exploration to following step by step procedures. We have found that giving some choices between following simple guidelines (such as use your hands, feet, knees, hips and elbows to show the rhythm of this song) and total free choice to explore a variety of selected music works best at the beginning. As always some children have experienced dance outside the classroom and they become the leaders of their group, providing their expertise. We usually allow the children to work in the hallway just outside our classroom to minimize the noise in class, and to provide a space away from other students so that they will be less inhibited or bashful. Students are always given the choice between performing their dance at the end of meeting time (see daily schedule) or performing privately for the teacher. We have found that once students see one group perform, they want to do likewise, and groups improve as they learn from previous performers.

What you will need:
- assorted music
- CD or tape player
- some basic instructions or guidelines

The Drama Centre can take a different shape depending on the goal and the target age group. For younger children, it is often enough to have playhouse materials, dress-up clothes, and toys available for make-believe play. For a more focussed activity, students can be provided with hand-puppets, masks, or stick puppets and an assortment of favourite stories in script form. As students gain more experience with this genre they are encouraged to script their own plays and then critique their performances. In other instances, we have provided students with a setting, characters, and a problem for which they had to script a solution and then act the solution out. Whatever the format, the drama centre has been a favourite no matter the age.

What you will need:
- assorted dress-up clothes
- playhouse materials
- masks, puppets (hand and stick)
- multiple copies of commercially published plays
- paper and guidelines for script writing
- performance critiquing suggestions
- suggestions for staged problems on task cards

The Drawing Centre We believe that drawing is a skill in which all children can become accomplished, if taught the basics of drawing. When we haven't provided a drawing opportunity for a while, children often request one. There is a perceptible difference in children who are given the chance to draw and sketch. They become completely immersed in the project. They are very focused and we notice how relaxed they become. We give a brief lesson on a technique and then let students practise. We believe that children need some guidance, as very few are "naturals". Without some drawing lessons they tend to keep drawing that same flower, house and rainbow. They do not learn to really look at what they are drawing but draw what they think you want them to draw.

We provide a sketch book for each child that we make from recycled paper. We have bound these with a plastic ring binder, as we have access to that type of binding machine. Before we had such a machine we simply stapled them together and that worked fine. The advantage of binding the book is being able to add more pages to it as the need arises.

What you will need:
- several quality books on drawing and children
- a sketch book for each child

The Music Centre Music is a medium that seems to greatly affect all who hear it. We want children to be able to appreciate all music, whether it be classical, contemporary, folk, jazz, modern or traditional. We want them to be able to recognize common elements in a selection of a particular type of music. At this centre children can respond to the lyrics in music and suggest piggyback lyrics, where they write new words to an old song. They can draw or paint to a classical piece, where they respond in visual representation to the emotion or images inspired by that piece. We have had children compose their own songs with terrific pride. Children can explore basic rhythm at this centre, and use and investigate instruments borrowed from the school music room. Even the kindergarten room is happy to lend their rhythm instruments for children to experiment. Children can listen to music and identify some of the instruments used. Children can learn to use basic notation of music and learn to play the scale on a keyboard.

What you will need:
- CD/tape player
- variety of music selections
- task card
- report form

The Painting Centre While younger children in kindergarten and sometimes grade one get to paint on a fairly regular basis, it is often considered fairly frivolous for older children to paint regularly in their classrooms except for specific art projects. With a few simple lessons, students can learn about background, middle ground, foreground, horizon, reflection, blending of colours, pointillism, and other painting techniques. Teachers may wish to solicit the help of artists in the community to do a short series of lessons on painting. With each task card at the painting centre, we provide a sample(s) of the technique on which we are working. Children begin to examine what they see in a way they didn't before, they experience the joy of creation, and are given an important outlet of expression.

What you will need:
- a good paint easel
- a variety of paint and paint pots
- painting paper
- a variety of different paint brushes of different sizes
- a collection of art samples
- task cards

The Sculpture Centre Transferring images into three dimensions has been a fascinating challenge for our students. To do so they have to accurately observe what they want, and to shape the medium into what they have planned. They can create their own works of art and begin to play with form. We give our students guidelines and samples to follow so that they can create sculptures using different techniques. For example, one activity we had at this centre was to have children create pictures made from plasticine. Published books that have used this technique were prominently displayed so children can see the technique and see how they can create these pictures themselves. Also we have had children create a modern sculpture made out of recycled materials. This junk art was a favourite, as it allowed for total creativity.

What you will need:
- a variety of materials for making sculptures
- paint
- a collection of pictures of modern sculptures, and traditional sculptures
- task cards

The Toys Centre The value of play and its necessity in the development of language and symbolic thought has been well documented by theorists such as Piaget, Weininger, and Vygotsky. For younger children, in particular, play is of the utmost importance in their development. When watching young children play, one can hear the "self-talk" that occurs, which will later be internalized as the inner thoughts of that person. The experiences gained when playing also allow for social as well as intellectual development. Play has been called "the work of children", and children put tremendous energy and thinking into this activity.

What you will need:
- a variety of toys that will allow children the opportunity to explore different roles, and many different experiences. For example: a variety of small cars, trucks, airplanes, plush animals, dolls, dishes, housekeeping toys, cash register, simple costumes like a firefighter's hat, etc.

It is possible to include with the **The Art Centre** - Painting, Drawing, and Sculpture.

The Self and Society-related centres

The Canadiana Centre is mainly concerned with exploring various aspects of Canadian life. Though we explore history and geography at other centres, there are many points of interest to students regarding sports, famous Canadians, politics, the arts, technology, and literature which can be regularly accessed at this centre. In the past we focussed on a study of Canada for several months. Our students were able to pick up all kinds of Canadian facts over that time period.

A teacher had visited us and decided to take much of our model and adapt it to her grade 6 class in Quebec. She developed centres with her students, and they included a centre about Canada. Upon visiting these students near the end of the year, for some feedback, they reported that the Canadiana Centre had been among their favourites. With the receipt of rave reviews we decided to add it to our lineup and allow students to resurrect all that they had learned during our study of Canada, and to glean new Canadian information.

What you will need:
- resources on Canada
- brochures, booklets, and pamphlets produced by various government departments
- task cards
- various recording formats

The Cooking Centre provides a multisensory experience for children. We see cooking as both an art and a science. Not only do children have the opportunity to read and share information about food, they also look at chemical reactions in foods, observe a variety of changes, note the effects of precise measurements of certain ingredients. They can also explore new foods, and foods from other cultures. Students can explore the aesthetics of food display and presentation. Parent volunteers can provide the different perspective and ways of preparation that expand a child's view of the world. We take pleasure in noting that the joy of sharing the end products of work at this centre with one's classmates provides many happy moments.

What you will need:
- recipe cards, cookbooks (it is even better if you have small serving recipes)
- cooking utensils, measuring cups and spoons
- access to cooking appliances in the school

The History Centre gives children the opportunity to investigate local, national and world people and events from the past. For example, children have investigated prime ministers of Canada, famous women in history, famous scientists, etc. There is an ever increasing number of good quality historical books available. Children are often fascinated by the events of the past. Since the release of the movie, *Titanic*, children have been devouring the books about that event. Also, CD Roms, and access to the Internet are invaluable. When the topic has been researched the children use the information for developing a written report, poster, time line, or dramatic re-enactment.

What you will need:
- historical books, films, CD Roms
- long rolls of paper for time lines
- task cards
- report form

The Map & Globe Centre moves children around the earth, figuratively speaking. At it, students must identify direction, draw maps, read maps and globes using grids, learn about the equator, continents, oceans, countries, cities and related features. We try to use a variety of maps that include political maps, topographical maps, and maps which show population distribution, farming, resources or industry. Students learn how to use the symbol box or key on the maps. They sometimes provide challenges or a countdown clue to a country for other students to solve.

What you will need:
- many different maps, globes and atlases
- task cards

The Personal Well Being Centre Many things contribute to our personal well being, especially a healthy lifestyle. Children need to know about basic nutrition and health. At this centre, they explore and learn about what is needed for good health. They investigate the balance and selection of foods required to maintain a healthy body. They reflect on the importance of an active life style, and they become more knowledgeable about the human body and its systems.

What you will need:
- a variety of books and materials about health, the human body, importance of exercise, and healthy food, etc.
- charts, and information brochures from doctors and dentists, public health nurses, and offices
- models of the human body
- task cards
- report forms

The Personal Well Being Centre could include the concepts of the Cooking Centre.

Having read through these suggested centres, you are probably teeming with ideas. Once a teacher becomes proficient at this type of open-ended design for centres, the possibilities are limitless. Teachers naturally tap into their creativity and ingenuity as they review their students' curricular needs. Many ideas have also been inspired by our students. They feel proud to have that input. They begin to learn that the choices for learning are endless.

Once the centres are chosen and put into place, it is the classroom management and organization that needs to be refined in order to make classroom life sane and productive. We have some suggestions for management and organization that have served us well and we hope they will help others.

CHAPTER 8

CLASSROOM MANAGEMENT AND ORGANIZATION

Even if you're on the right track,
you will get run over if you just sit there.
— *WILL ROGERS*

In the end, the mind of the teacher is the most powerful influence in any classroom.
What she knows and believes about children
will create the atmosphere affecting their learning.
What she does in every single situation originates in what she thinks.
— *ALICE YARDLEY*

Classroom management and organization strategies are the backbone of teaching which hold the class and teaching practices together. They are also what helps everyone keep their sanity in an ever-stressing world. With well-devised management strategies, students become a cohesive group, respectful of others and their property. They are responsible for themselves and caring for one another. Many of the strategies we use instil a sense of ownership in the students so that they are empowered in the decision-making and the maintenance of "our" classroom. When students are empowered they feel a sense of control over themselves, (we really stress self-control!) and their surroundings. Such empowerment also boosts their self-confidence to be contributing members of the class. All of this leads to a reduced number of behaviour problems, and optimal learning.

Some organization strategies to put into place

Included here are some strategies which the dynamic model teacher will benefit from using. Wherever possible we have provided helpful blackline masters, which can be found in the appendices.

Putting students into groups The whole class is divided into heterogeneous groups, usually five to six students depending on the total class size. This is done by evenly mixing ages, gender, abilities, and special needs. These groups are the "learning teams". They are useful for a variety of reasons. Students work in their groups during must-do activity centre time. When the teacher needs to manage the class in smaller numbers, the groups are easily called upon. When it is necessary for the whole class to sit at their tables we request that they sit with their groups. When it is easier from a management point of view (such as for lunchtime, or reflective writing) and it doesn't impinge on their learning processes, we use the table groupings. They are not permanently fixed nor used all day. There are many occasions when exceptions are made since some children need to move off to a quieter spot or a few students may want to put their heads together to explore an idea. Periodically throughout the year we make changes to members of each group. Students also put in writing requests for changes. When we see a legitimate need for the change we usually accede the request.

Shape labels for groups Each group table is labelled with a shape made of coloured bristol board and laminated. The shape then can be hung from the ceiling above the table and the names of the group members are recorded with erasable marker on the shape, for anyone to see. When you have eight groups or more (as we do in a double classroom) everyone is grateful to see a point of reference to discern group members' names. See Blackline Masters #9-11 for group shapes.

Group members chart It is extremely useful for planning purposes and for referring to at a glance, to have the list of students at each group on one chart. One copy can be displayed on the wall and another can be kept in the teacher's record book. See Blackline Master #12 for a blank group members chart.

Group leaders Each week we assign one member of each group to be the group leader. The group leader's duties are varied in scope. They include assisting with handing out papers to each table, gathering the required bins for centres, reminding people to do certain jobs, collecting work at the end of a session, doing table inspections and being available for impromptu jobs. We use the group members chart to track who is the group leader for the week. Since the chart is usually posted at the front with the other jobs, calendar, and meeting info, we use an

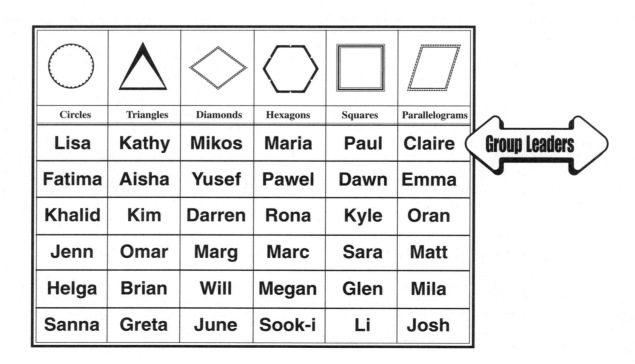

Circles	Triangles	Diamonds	Hexagons	Squares	Parallelograms
Lisa	Kathy	Mikos	Maria	Paul	Claire
Fatima	Aisha	Yusef	Pawel	Dawn	Emma
Khalid	Kim	Darren	Rona	Kyle	Oran
Jenn	Omar	Marg	Marc	Sara	Matt
Helga	Brian	Will	Megan	Glen	Mila
Sanna	Greta	June	Sook-i	Li	Josh

Group Leaders

arrow that points to a row of the group members chart and move the arrow each week on a rotational basis. We also have a poster that outlines the duties of the group leader for easy reference. See Blackline Master #43 for the duties of the group leader poster.

Book buckets   Since students do not have individual desks with storage space, we provide them with a sturdy bucket in which the variety of notebooks, writing folders, and work logs can be stored and easily retrieved. We find the standard plastic washbasin is sturdy and the books can stand up in this container. We have used two different sorting methods for organizing the various materials.

    1. Sorting by group - Each group is given a group bucket in which to house their books and folders. The bucket, each member's books, and storage shelf are labelled with the group shape for easy sorting.

    2. Sorting by subject area book buckets - As an alternative to having group buckets, we have tried sorting books by subject area rather than by groups. The buckets are labelled with the subject area or name of book.

There are advantages to both methods and the choice is a matter of preference. When sorting by subject, you will not have the quick access to each group's books that you do when books are kept in a group bucket. However, we get around that by having group leaders hand out books a minute or two before they are needed. For some reason, there seemed to be a higher number of lost notebooks when we were using the group buckets. The concept of the group buckets makes sense because the groups have access to their whole set of books quickly. A combination of the two sorting systems may be a solution, whereby a limited set of notebooks are kept in the group buckets and other items, such as sketch books, writing folders, reading logs, and math logs are stored in their own buckets. See Blackline Master #63 for subject area bucket labels.

Student work kits   Students need a place to keep pencils, erasers, glue sticks, and pencil crayons. A work kit is just a plastic box with a lid, approx. 20cm. x 15cm. They are taken by each student to their different centres or work stations and when they are not in use, can easily be stacked in the middle of the group table. They cost approximately a dollar at any business supply store or large department store.

Student mailboxes   For the purpose of sending home newsletters, notices, and finished work, individual student mailboxes are handy. If you aren't fortunate enough to have a carpenter available, you can use the twelve-bottle capacity liquor boxes turned over on their sides. The exterior can easily be covered with plastic self-stick MacTac™. Label the front lip of each compartment with the student names. As an alternative you can use 48 oz. juice cans, stacked in pyramid fashion and fastened together. It is a good idea for the teacher to have a mailbox as

juice cans

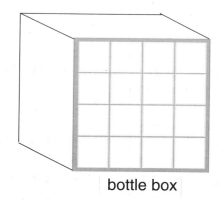

bottle box

well, so she/he won't be inundated with notes held in her/his face first thing in the morning. Instead the students can put them in the teacher's mailbox slot. See Blackline Master #65 for small blank name plates.

Must-do list On the front board at the meeting area, is located the list of must-do centres and the corresponding group which must complete that centre for that day. The group shapes are miniatures fixed on the board with a magnet. The centre labels are duplicates of the graphics on the check-in system.

Must-do Centres:

Big Books Centre | Correspondence Centre | Grammer Examine Centre | Drawing Centre | Map and Globe Centre | Dance Centre

Groups:

Groups move one space per day in this direction.

The shape labels move to the next centre each day. The centre cards stay stationary but are changed easily when the centres are changed for the next round of must-do's.

Work logs This is the student tracking system used to follow what centre activities have been commenced and completed by individuals. Each of the students fill in the spaces and the logs are checked at the end of each week.

At one time, we kept the whole group's work logs on a clipboard labelled with the group shape and stored in the group bucket. The group leader was responsible during activity time for reminding everyone to sign their work logs. Then we had individual work logs kept in a book bag which was kept in each group bucket. They seemed to get lost frequently. We now keep all the work logs from September onwards in a duotang for each student with the current month on top. The duotangs are kept in a work log bucket. This storage system for the work logs seems to be working the best for us so far.

The benefits of the work log are two-fold. First, the student can tell at a glance what work is completed and what needs to be finished. Second, the teacher can check the student's work log against the entries in her centres binder to see if the student's work has been completed and recorded. For more detail on the work log see Chapter 9: Evaluation and Authentic Assessment. See Blackline Master #89 for blank work log.

Work Log	○ △ ◇ ⬡ ▢ ▱	Name	Kathy			

Period beginning October 10, 2005   **Period ending** November 8, 2005

Day	Centre Name	Activity Name	Performance	Score	Finished?	Checked
Mon.	Science	types of seeds	2	3	Y	✓
Tues.	Math	place value	3	3	N	•
Wed.	Word study	weather puzzle	3	4	Y	✓
Thurs.						
Fri.						
Mon.						
Tues.						
Wed.						
Thurs.						
Fri.						
Mon.						
Tues.						
Wed.						
Thurs.						
Fri.						
Mon.						
Tues.						
Wed.						
Thurs.						
Fri.						

Level of performance: 1 to 5   Signed off by:

Job list This a list of jobs or tasks that students are responsible for each day. Some are comprised of authentic learning events and others are simply classroom maintenance jobs. These change daily and are located on the front board near the meeting area.

The students' names are listed in a single column and mounted on the front chalkboard or white board. Most often these boards are magnetic. The jobs are listed on individual arrows with magnets on the back of each. Each arrow points to the assigned student's name for the day. The arrows are moved down one spot each day so that students know when to anticipate each job and often look forward to their turn. We encourage them to do jobs first thing in the morning so that they are prepared for the meeting, when they will report on their job, if appropriate. See Blackline Master #58-62 for the job arrows.

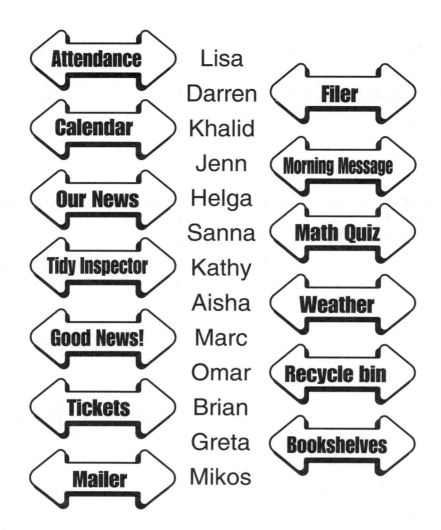

Attendance · Lisa
Darren · Filer
Calendar · Khalid
Jenn · Morning Message
Our News · Helga
Sanna · Math Quiz
Tidy Inspector · Kathy
Aisha · Weather
Good News! · Marc
Omar · Recycle bin
Tickets · Brian
Greta · Bookshelves
Mailer · Mikos

Bins, double labels As much as possible, all materials, manipulatives and supplies are kept in labelled bins, buckets, or baskets. Then their places on the shelves are also labelled so there is never any question where an item belongs. For consistency, we use the same coloured card stock to make all of our labels around the room. When visiting teachers or students are in, they can contribute to the overall maintenance of the classroom with very little difficulty.

Book borrowing These slips are made available at the Book Resource Centre so students can borrow books from our classroom overnight. Once the slip is filled out, it is placed in the student's name pocket where it is readily visible. When the teacher notices that there is a book borrowing slip in the pocket, a gentle reminder can be given to that student. See the Blackline Master #104 for the book borrowing slips.

Book Borrowing

I borrowed this book from the class Book/Resource Centre:

Title: _____

_____

Author: _____

Borrower: _____

Date: _____

Sorting work buckets For ease of marking and tracking work, students are required to put finished work in the corresponding bucket. The buckets are located as near as possible to the teacher's work space. Buckets are labelled as follows for easy sorting:

· finished math
· finished science

- finished work
- work to be filed (work that is marked and to be returned to the group bucket)
- work to be mailed (work that should be taken home)
- unfinished work
- work being published (needs to be bound or illustrated)
- projects in progress
- writing being published
- library book return

See Blackline Master #64 for the sorting work bucket labels.

Assortment of notebooks Notebooks are used to keep student work accessible and organized. Students sometimes glue related papers into their notebooks or write directly on the pages. Students reflect on their collection of work over time and can see progress when they are able to review it. Too often when loose papers are used, things get lost or they are left at home, making difficult to review learning or go back and catch up. The following is a list of the notebooks we use:

- **Math log** - used for recording during math-related centres and during whole group math lessons.
- **Learning log** - a personal journal used to reflect on such things as setting goals and learning.
- **Science log** - used for recording during science-related centres and during whole group science lessons.
- **Sketchbook** - used for drawing practice, and sketching out poster or painting ideas.
- **Language record book** - used for recording during language-related centres and during whole group language lessons.
- **Everything book** - used for everything else that doesn't fit into the math, science, language categories. It also comes in handy when one of the other notebooks can't be found or is left at home.
- **Spelling record book** - used for practising spelling exercises and to record homework study lists, and personal word lists.
- **Anything book** - used to do anything in such as cartoon drawing, play tic tac toe, try out a writing idea, play hangman on a rainy day. This book is not for any evaluative purpose but simply a private place where students can do as they wish.

Student writing folder Every student has their own two-pocket writing folder of which there are numerous commercial varieties available. There are luxury models which come in plastic and have the writing process printed on them and there are the plain Janes which are simply light cardboard and come in different colours. Once we made our own from recycled poster board. No matter what model you have available to you, the important thing is that they have pockets and are durable enough to last at least one year. We have always laminated the cardboard versions which extends their life considerably.

Student portfolios In recent years there have been an abundance of materials produced to facilitate the production of student portfolios. We have found these resources to be valuable. (See the Bibliography - Evaluation and Assessment section for some recommended publications on portfolios.) We have worked through a number of scenarios to get where we are now with our portfolios. The storage system we are now using was decided school-wide but the process of collecting and reflecting is tailored by each teacher. It is important to have the storage system ready for the beginning of school so this learning process can be introduced at the onset and some valuable baseline samples can be collected. We use hanging files (one for each student) each of which holds a set of six coloured files, one colour for each strand: the Arts, Language, Math, Science/Tech, Self & Society, and French. For more evaluation strategies see Chapter 9: Evaluation and Authentic Assessment.

Conference/Interview in progress sign Students like to know that they have the teacher's full attention when they are engaged in a writing conference or an interview. For that reason it is practical to have available a "conference/interview in progress" sign which can be displayed and works to limit interruptions. If someone is about to interrupt a conference, the conferencing student simply holds up the sign to send a clear message to the intruder. See Blackline Masters #56-57 for the signs.

Art gallery wall When planning your room environment try to incorporate space for an art gallery wall. We found the hallway walls just outside work well as our art gallery space. Students as artists need a space to proudly display their artwork. We make name plates with captions for artwork and students are encouraged to sign and date all artwork in the bottom corner.

Our writers' wall Students are given their own display space for writing over which they have control. No matter the level of ability, students all have the right to display some writing thereby eliminating the stigma of never having work which is good enough to be put out in full view. For full details on construction and use see Chapter 9: Evaluation and Authentic Assessment.

Important message board At the front of the room, in the general vicinity of the meeting area, we have a section of our chalkboard designated for important messages and a smaller section to record absences. Notes are sometime attached here if someone has to leave early. Messages from the principal are posted. Missing homework or anything else we want to relay to the students such as a particular centre being closed for a period of time is written here.

> **Important messages**
> for
> Monday, May 11, 1998
>
> You need to take home your Reading to Go.
>
> Jessica has lost her sunglasses.
>
> The art centre is closed for 1 week.
>
> > Mohamed, you have to meet your mother in the office at 3:00

Poster displays We have some wonderful commercially produced posters which provide students with relevant information in all curricular areas. These are put on display as close to the relevant centre as possible. They provide models for those at the poster project centre. The poster project centre is a popular centre which has students producing a great variety of quality posters and critiquing them. Part of the learning process is displaying posters for a wider audience outside of the classroom. We make use of space in the hallway or around the office to display student work as often as we can.

Class information posters are on display near the meeting area for easy reference when reviewing class procedures such as:

- **The No-clowning Carpet Credo** - outlining appropriate behaviour for meeting time.

- **Rainy Day Activities** - indoor recess choices.

- **Procedures for doing must-do centres** - outlining the steps for doing must-do centres.

- **You should tell on someone when:** - outlining when it is appropriate to reports someone's actions.

- **If you have a problem with someone...** - outlining steps for dealing with a bothersome person.

- **Good Day!** - reminders for beginning the school day.

- **Project/Interview Day Procedures:** - steps for what to do on project/interview days.

- **How to do quality work** - guidelines for doing quality work.

- **Lunchtime behaviour** - outlining appropriate behaviour for lunchtime.

- **Champion Classroom Cleaners** - guidelines for keeping the classroom clean.

See Blackline Masters #42-52 for set of class information posters.

Answer can/treasure box When students have the answer to the daily quiz recorded on a piece of paper, they deposit it into the answer can. Students are encouraged to answer the quiz every day. At the end of the week names are drawn out of the can. Students whose names are drawn are allowed to choose a prize out of the treasure box. This is a box of simple treasures we keep such as bookmarks, marbles, stickers, pencils, plastic rings, buttons etc. Often we draw most of the names from the answer can to encourage participation.

Washroom "tombstones" With so much going on in our classroom it is easy to loose track of where someone might be. Since children are given over the responsibility of their bodily functions at a young age (most hopefully by the age of two), we do not like to have them revert when they come to school. When they have a need to go to the washroom they use what has been dubbed the "tombstone" to notify where they have gone. Since we have designated washrooms for boys and girls our signs are also designated by gender. This wooden marker is placed on their work space, or table with their name ticket in the pocket. Since students are given the freedom to choose when they will leave the room, we have a discussion ahead of time as to what times would be best to choose to leave. Choosing to go to the washroom during a lesson, for instance, would not be the best time as the student would be missing important information. However, when there is an emergency, leaving the room does take precedence.

Library pass Because we like to have the students choose when they might like to go to the school library to pick out books for home reading, we have an added pocket on our check-in system for library passes. If students wish to research a particular topic they complete a library request form, get approval and take the pass with the information to the librarian so the librarian will know their specific needs. See Blackline Master #103 for library request forms and Blackline Master #6 for the library pass.

. . . .

When these management and organization strategies are in place, they often inspire other ideas by the students and teacher. The critical question when implementing these strategies is, "What strategy design will give more responsibility to the students and make learning more accessible?" Some of the simplest ideas can be helpful in meeting these goals.

Again, keep in mind that you can only take one step at a time.

CHAPTER 9

EVALUATION AND AUTHENTIC ASSESSMENT

A mistake is simply another way of doing things.
— KAY GRAHAM

We don't make mistakes. We just have learnings.
— ANNE WILSON SCHAEF

It is a bad plan that admits of no modification.
— PUBLILIUS SYRUS

A Change in Perspective

Before you begin delivering the curriculum, it is important to have a clear understanding of the assessment and evaluation procedures that you will employ. In child-centred, literacy-based, process-driven programs there is a need to have forms of assessment and evaluation that are authentic i.e., assessment that assesses learning in the context of real classroom activities rather than in the form of standardized and teacher-made written tests. In the dynamic classroom there is a push towards authentic learning i.e., children are responsible decision-makers and have learning experiences based on real life events. How we teach has to match how we assess the students and the programme we run. Such a match is vital in the dynamic teaching model.

For a long time now, teachers have recognized the need for alternatives in assessment. There are many current writers in the field of literacy and other areas of education who address the issues of testing, assessment, and evaluation. (Please see the Evaluation and Assessment section from the References and Recommended Reading list, p. I) It is necessary to incorporate assessment systems with the work of everyday teaching and learning in what is referred to as authentic assessment.

When we are asked what our school experiences were like in terms of assessment or evaluation, most of us would reply that we wrote tests. Today assessment and evaluation continue to evolve just as teaching practices do.

Assessment activities are beginning to look very different from the traditional Friday quiz or unit test that we had in each subject. Before describing some of the authentic assessment tools in our class and how we use them, we should differentiate between testing, assessment, and evaluation.

Defining testing, assessment, and evaluation

Testing is an outcome measure used to compare children against prescribed expectations and tends to be summative in nature. Assessment is a formative evaluation of the individual student performance, of what has been learned, what needs to be learned, and how children are learning (Strickland & Morrow, 1989). Formative assessment occurs frequently and throughout the formation of the child's learning and tends to be qualitative. Summative assessment occurs at the summation of the learning and gives a quantitative measure of the total of a child's learning. Assessment occurs on many levels and uses a variety of instruments and strategies (Teale, Hiebert, & Chittendon,1987). Evaluation incorporates both testing and student assessment to determine whether a programme, in all its interconnected components, meets its objectives. This approach requires the judgment of the teacher as evaluation expert.

Evaluation goes beyond testing and student assessment and considers other factors. For example, it is important to analyze the learning environment which is provided — room arrangements, and the quality and accessibility of materials (Strickland & Morrow, 1989).

A need for process-oriented assessment

The perspective of assessment that has been slowly emerging has precipitated the development of some very practical approaches to how we assess children. We no longer care only about the product of their learning in our assessment; we also focus on the processes of students' learning. In other words in our assessment practices we are as concerned with how children learn and their own thinking about their learning as we are concerned with what they learn. Assessment should be process-oriented not product-oriented (Harp, 1988; Johnston, 1987).

Teachers are already heavily burdened with growing curricular demands. The last thing anyone wants to hear about is another requirement added to the work of teaching. However, assessment is an absolutely necessary component of the work of teaching. It is valuable for more than just informing the teacher, student, and parents of the student's progress and literacy development. Student assessment is a subcategory of evaluation. It is felt that the most important goal of all educational evaluation is to achieve optimal instruction for all children (Johnston, 1987). We should always be reflecting on and investigating our teaching practices and for that purpose we require appropriate assessment methods.

Authentic assessment methods are an integral part of the teaching day. Teachers practising authentic assessment incorporate a variety of methods into their daily teaching. "Kid-watching", reading interviews, running records, portfolio assessment, student-led conferencing, and writing samples are all part of the daily authentic assessment toolkit. These methods are part of the real work of teaching, and are relevant to the process of learning. Without daily attention to assessment on all levels - self, student, and programme - teaching is incomplete.

Organization and strategies

For assessment to be real and valid it requires organization and integration. Organization is necessary to integrate assessment into the daily routines of instruction and learning. Once the organizational framework is laid out the students can facilitate the assessment process with certain tasks of their own. The key to starting out is to keep it simple and efficient. It is important to balance how much time is spent using a particular assessment tool with how much information it is providing.

Literature focussed on literacy development, in the 1980's, provides us with numerous alternatives in the area of assessment such as: checklists, running records, reading inventories, reader response, writing samples, self-reports, peer evaluation, "kid-watching", and reading conferences, to name a few (Au, Scheu, Kawakami, & Herman, 1990; Chittendon & Courtney, 1989; Flood & Lapp, 1989; Matthews, 1990; Valencia, 1990).

It can be overwhelming to attempt to integrate all of these methods into your teaching practices. Often, the biggest question we are asked is "How do you collect assessment data and find the time to do it all?" The organizational strategies we put into practice should assist you in making decisions about your evaluation process. Incorporating the following strategies will provide the organization which will maximize efficiency and minimize teacher stress. We are not providing the theoretical framework of how to conduct assessments and evaluations but rather the organizational systems which will provide you with the opportunities to conduct authentic assessments. For detailed evaluation practices, look to our recommended reading list on evaluation. There are numerous volumes on this topic which we have found to be influential in our development as educators.

Before each school year begins we prepare our chosen assessment tools. At the very least we lay out the types of assessment strategies we will employ. In our earlier years, we began with a few key assessment "tools" and then over some years incorporated more of these methods. They provide us with very complete pictures of what each child has accomplished, and how they did it, and how well they did it. Once this is in place, report cards, parent interviews and reviewing our whole programme is a relatively easy process as we have such an accurate picture of each child and where he/she stands in relationship to the programme and the environment. We can also easily determine where changes need to be made in our delivery of curriculum and in the physical environment of our classroom.

Teacher record keeping

We use large, 3-ring binders to organize and house the recording of student assessment data. Different types of forms are photocopied in a different colour for each category of assessment making for easy reference in each of the binders.

1. Student evaluation binder
This binder is first sectioned off into the main categories of:

A) **Observations**
B) **Language**
C) **Math**
D) **Science/Tech**
E) **The Arts**

All forms and binder cover pages are available in the Blackline Masters section. See Blackline Masters #16-37.)

The sections consist of the following:

A) Observations are records of "kid-watching", anecdotal notes of individual students which are taken regularly. One "at-a-glance" type sheet is maintained for each student. There is a small box provided for each child, to record what the teacher can observe about a child's learning. A different focus can be taken at different times of the year. The date is recorded for each observation.

Grade 2, 3 & 4   *B. Szatanski*

Student Evaluation Records

Math, Spelling, Reading, Writing, Res

Observations		Name:	

B) The **Language** section is comprised of four subsections.
- a) Notes on reading progress are made on the **Reading Interview** sheet, one for each student. The date, title, and level of the book is recorded as well as assessment notes which involve the use of running records or miscue analysis.
- b) A similar device is used for **Writing Interviews** which assess the writing process. One form is made per student as shown on the following page.
- c) **Ongoing writing projects** such as animal research, research projects, and story writing are tracked on class list sheets according to the date started, date finished, and topic. It is easy to see at a glance at which stage every student is with their writing projects.
- d) **Class list records** are also used to keep track of spelling, the number of reading entries, and any other related data collection.

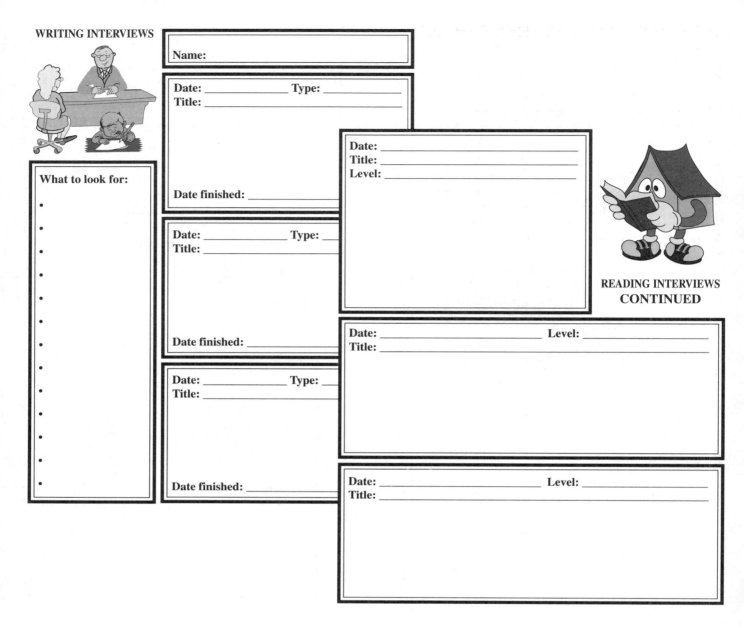

WRITING INTERVIEWS

Name:

Date: _____ Type: _____
Title: _____

Date finished: _____

Date: _____ Type: _____
Title: _____

Date finished: _____

Date: _____ Type: _____
Title: _____

Date finished: _____

What to look for:

•
•
•
•
•
•
•
•
•
•

Date: _____
Title: _____
Level: _____

**READING INTERVIEWS
CONTINUED**

Date: _____ Level: _____
Title: _____

Date: _____ Level: _____
Title: _____

C) The **Math** section has two types of data collection:

  a) The **Math Interview** form, one per student.
  b) **Class list records** keep track of unit tests, practice worksheets, completed homework, etc.

D) Both the **Science/Tech** section and

E) **The Arts** section have class list records to keep track of work done in those strands.

2. Must-do centre marking binder

In a separate binder we record the progress students make on must-do centres.
At the end of each activity time, students hand in their must-do work to the corresponding tub.
The work is assessed daily and recorded on class list sheets which have the must-do centres as headings. These sheets are categorized in language, math, science, technology/multimedia, self and society, and art centres for easier access. Short anecdotal notes are made in these boxes referring to progress and quality or sometimes just a numerical value depending on the item.

Grade 2, 3 & 4   B. Szatanski

Must-do Centre Marking

3. Personal records binder

This binder contains a record sheet for each child which lists the birth date, address, home phone, and mother's and father's names and work phone numbers. Attached to this information is a record of the **Communication History**. Whenever a phone call is made, a note sent home, or an interview is conducted, it is recorded. We also keep a copy of any special testing and a copy of each term report in that same binder. We have a lot of individual student information housed in one binder for ease of reference and for use preparing for parent interviews. See page 72.

Student generated data, demonstrations and performances

The work log is used to track the daily tasks at activity centres by individual students. This form holds up to a month's worth of work. Because students may choose one of three to four tasks at a given centre they are required to record the centre name and the activity name

Student Personal Records

Personal Records

Communication History

Student Name _____

Birthdate _____

Address _____

_____

Home Phone _____

Mother's Phone _____

Father's Phone _____

on the log. Both students and teachers can follow up on the unfinished work noted on the work log. Students are also required to do some reflection and evaluation of the quality of their work habits and results. They must give themselves a score out of 5 under the column heading "Performance" on their work log. They are given guidelines as to what they are assessing on the poster entitled, "Level of Performance" which is glued into the front cover of each student's work log duotang for easy reference. If you are teaching in the early primary grades you can adapt the language to suit younger students and include a picture code. We also provide our own assessment on a column on the work log as to what we have observed during centre time. At the end of each week, we cross check our records in our must-do tracking binder before a student can be signed off for free choice. This assessment activity serves several purposes as it provides a cross check for the teacher to see if work is completed and provides the opportunity for every student to reflect on their own daily work, and to make judgments on time management. — "Will I take this home tonight to finish for homework and then have free choice on catch-up day when my teacher has checked my work log, or will I wait until I'm told to do this during 'catch-up day?" — We do lots of modelling for students regarding making such decisions when we think out loud with them. (See Blackline Master #90 for Level of Performance poster.)

When we have a variety of activities or centres during math or science time blocks, for an extended period of time we use the subject-specific work log to help us track the students' progress. On these work logs we ask students to reflect on their learning in a slightly different way from the integrated work log. However you design the work log, it will become apparent that having students track their progress by "signing in" and verifying what they have done, adds a note of validity to the work of learning and makes tracking a lot easier for the teacher.

Student portfolios are maintained by the students as much as possible. However, there must be in place a tightly monitored organization system. As mentioned in the previous chapter, we use a storage system which requires a file cabinet, hanging file folders, and files. Whatever storage system you decide upon, the following organization strategies will still be usable. We have the portfolio storage system ready for the first week of school and the students start out with the following:

Table of contents card - is used to assist students in organizing the contents of their portfolios.

The criteria for assessing your
Level of Performance

After you have completed your job, ask yourself:

1. Did you remain on task for the whole time?

2. Did you use all resources available to you?

3. Did you organize yourself and your materials?

4. Did you review your work for corrections and additions (remember date, centre, and title).

5. Does your work look polished?
   (neat writing and coloured drawings)

If you answered yes to :

1 or 2 questions	—	fair
3 or 4 questions	—	good
all 5 questions	—	Super!

Give yourself a score out of 5.

Reading record /conference log - lists books read, responses, conferences with peers or teacher, and is kept in a duotang. (We also have a Hypercard stack version of this for each student on their AppleShare computer file.)

Published works list - lists all published work by the student, the type of writing, the title, and the date finished.

Setting personal goals - set at the beginning of each term.

Looking back on the term - a reflection of progress, done at the end of each term.

Portfolio Pride and envelope - selected work is chosen and reflected upon for specified reasons, and attached to an explanatory note with the heading "Portfolio Pride". These selections are kept together inside a large envelope also marked Portfolio Pride.

Portfolios are kept where students have ready access to store or retrieve their work whenever possible. Next to the storage place, we keep a file box where selected work can be placed for filing later when it isn't convenient to do so immediately. Sometimes filing can be done by a parent volunteer or a student helper. See Blackline Masters #91-93 for all these portfolio forms.

Learning log - Right from the beginning of the year, students are given prompts to: reflect

PORTFOLIO PRIDE

This selection was made for _Fatima_ 's Portfolio.   Date _May 3, 2005_

I included this work in my portfolio because _it was the first time I wrot an experiment report and I liked it._

I did it when _we were studying about different clouds and made a cloud in a bowl._

I learned _that warm air condenses and turns to rain when it comes in contact with cold._

on their learning and their experiences within the classroom environment, to set goals, and evaluate their progress. In our classroom, the learning log has taken over the traditional journal. Having tried different types of personal expression formats we've found this is the most effective method to facilitate reflection and growth.

Math musings Our delivery of mathematics concepts and skills has changed with the development of an integrated, hands-on approach. This approach emphasizes number sense, spatial sense, and problem-solving as integral to all of the strands in math. With the understanding that math is language-based we have come to conclude that children need to be able to express verbally and demonstrate their understanding of the various math concepts through the use of manipulatives, diagrams, charts, graphs, and calculations. To get students moving in that direction, we use a journal-type writing strategy before starting a math unit of learning and at the conclusion of the unit. We use a spiral bound book of blank paper entitled "Math Musings". A variety of prompts are given to get the students started. Each entry begins with the date and a topic title. For instance, at the beginning of a unit on geometry the following would be used:

> March 3, 1998
>
> About Shapes and Solids
>
> I know that...

and then part way through the learning another entry may be made:

```
                              March 9, 1998

        About Shapes and Solids

        The difference between
        shapes and solids are...
```

And to conclude the unit the final entry could look like this:

```
                              March 16, 1998

        About Shapes and Solids

        I learned...
```

Students are also encouraged to elaborate on their writing through the use of diagrams, charts, graphs, and calculations. This approach enhances the communication of their understanding.

Update/sign-up lists The following types of information are recorded by the students. These lists are kept on clipboards hung on hooks in an accessible space.

- **Class published books** update is a list that all students add to whenever they have published a book. This list is then printed out on the computer and posted on the wall. The challenge is to get the posted running list to reach the floor!

- **Animal Research Update,** and **Research Projects Update** are sign-up sheets for students to record the topics they are currently working on. This is useful for the teacher and for fellow students to note especially when resources and research materials need to be shared. See example on page 76.

- **The conference sign-up sheet** is for individuals to indicate that they would like a conference appointment. In this way teachers don't lose track of students and can allot time as the list grows.

See Blackline Masters #80-83 for these update/sign-up sheets.

Everyone can see the growing body of work produced by the whole class as these lists are visible to everyone and up-to-date. This acts as a motivating feature.

Our writers' wall is set up in a prominent space in the classroom or in a visible display area in the corridor. Every member including the teachers have their own space (approximately 10" x 13"), with a nameplate (10" x 2"). A brightly coloured sturdy cardboard with a large butterfly clip at the top is permanently mounted in the space. It acts like a clipboard so that

CLASS ANIMAL RESEARCH UPDATE

Your name	Name of Animal	Finish Date
Darren	bear	Oct. 13
Aisha	Deer	Nov. 10
Peter	wolf	Dec. 6
Brandon	Lion	Jan. 6

pieces of writing can be added or removed with relative ease. If it is possible, make the space for each child one that they can easily access themselves. Students increase their ownership of the space by decorating their nameplate and choosing the colour. If clips are not available you can use wallpaper as backing for the whole bulletin board and separate each student's space with ribbon. Work can be attached with pins or thumbtacks. Whenever students have some writing which has been completed they may add it if they wish to our writers' wall. Note the word "add" because with the clip you can add writing to the wall. (This is not done as easily with pins or thumbtacks.) This method is important. The students experience a sense of accomplishment seeing their work accumulate. This method is more efficient than removing and replacing pieces of writing. When the space is full and needs to be cleared, the teacher and student can take this time to conference. Together you can examine the progress made over the course of the writing. At conferences, it is decided which selections are to be placed in the personal portfolio and which ones can be taken home.

The students are primarily responsible for the maintenance of the writers' wall. Before a piece of writing is placed on the wall, it must be date stamped so a date stamp should be available for the students' use. Items are usually placed chronologically on the wall, with the most recent writing placed on top. Not every piece of writing will necessarily be placed on the wall. Students may wish to take some writing home but as they almost always write more than one draft of a story they can place one on the wall. When writing is displayed in the corridor, children are aware that there is another audience for their writing so they know that there is a place to showcase their work and that space is not only reserved for the "best in the class". They are eager to share their work because of this. They take the responsibility of choosing which selections to display. Another responsibility of each student is to stamp their work with a "rough draft" stamp or "final draft" stamp. This changes the expectations for spelling and neatness when the writing process is assessed. Often students return to the wall for a rough draft, which had been there for awhile, in order to complete the writing process to publication stage.

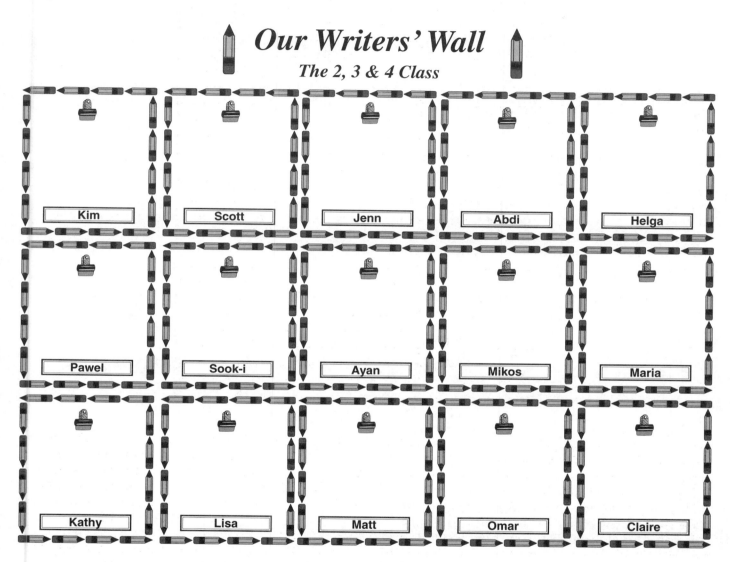

Our Writers' Wall

The 2, 3 & 4 Class

Kim Scott Jenn Abdi Helga

Pawel Sook-i Ayan Mikos Maria

Kathy Lisa Matt Omar Claire

   In any given week, a teacher can see at a glance who has been productive in their writing and who may need some encouragement and help. It is recommended that writing conferences take place every month so that the students space may be cleared, and that selection can be made for the student's portfolio. By designing the framework and placing the responsibility of maintenance of the writers' wall on the students, you have a system which fulfills several purposes and is efficient. It is one assessment strategy which not only allows the student to reflect on his/her progress, but also provides data for the teacher to reflect on the efficacy of the literacy programme as well as on the achievement of learning outcomes. See Blackline Master #67 for large blank name plates for the writers' wall and art gallery.

   The Art Gallery functions much the same as the Writers' Wall. It is not placed on a bulletin board but utilizes wall space in the hallway. The background uses the standard large sheets of construction paper (24 x 36 inches). Then a frame is created by using strips of coloured construction paper along the edges of the background. A name plate is mounted at the bottom of the frame. The art gallery is a permanent display outside of our classroom and is very handsome. The art gallery serves a greater purpose than that of just looking nice. Students take pride in their accomplishments and don't feel judged against their peers when they have equal opportunity to have things on display. It is a quick way to check who needs a little push to get certain art projects completed. At the beginning of the year, the whole class is given time to complete a family portrait and then later a self-portrait. These are the first pieces to be mounted in the art gallery. Later art work is generated through the different art centres. Artists are always required to sign and date their work. When the art work is removed from the gallery, selections are made for the portfolios. Students are given opportunities to write critiques on their classmates' work. This adds another dimension of evaluation.

Aisha Kamba

The six box review At the end of a science-based chunk of study, students are often given a "six box review". Between twelve and twenty related topics are listed on the board from which students choose six, for which they write everything they know. Students are encouraged to include labelled diagrams. We provide the students with two sizes of review sheets. (Available in the Blackline Masters #95-97) The smaller six box review sheet is used at the beginning of the year or for younger, beginner students who are not used to this type of open-ended assessment. When the students find they have a lot to write, as older students do, you can switch to the larger two-sided six box review form. These are kept in the student portfolio for review.

Student published book display
On one of our forages through used furniture, junk, and castoffs, we came across a metal commercial music book display stand. Books are placed on the stand facing forward so that they are easily seen. We now use this stand for our students' publications. It provides a pleasing display right outside our door. This type of bookstand is available in education catalogues, made of wood or plastic-coated metal.

March 12, 1998	REVIEW	by: Aisha Kamba
All About Weather		
The water cycle The sun heats up the water. It evaporates and rises, then condenses.	Types of clouds	
What is lightening?	How a tornado is formed	
Forecasting the weather	Weather instruments	

We have often noticed older students casually picking up a student-authored book and getting great enjoyment out of reading it. It also comes in handy when parents are waiting for their appointment time during parent-teacher interviews.

From time to time, students are given the opportunity to choose a classmate's book and write a critical review of it. The review is then read to the whole class by the reviewer and the author of the book is given a chance to respond. We have noted that the responses of the authors are usually very positive even in the light of some critical comments and suggested changes for the writing. They are usually quite proud that someone has chosen their book to showcase in this way.

Our Class Newsletter Once a month one of the learning groups is responsible for putting together Our Class Newsletter. This is an authentic method of student self-evaluation in which they are eager to take part.

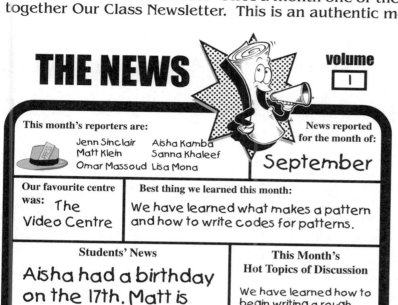

The students gather information from their classmates as well as reflect on their own month's learning. They are provided with a blank framework on which to write their rough draft. (See Blackline Masters #98-99 for a blank newsletter outline.) The contents include the following types of information:

Hot topics of discussion
Favourite centre
Activity centres for the month
Students' news
School wide news
Teachers' news
Best thing learned
Book of the month
Favourite poem of the month
Favourite new word
Favourite joke of the month
Important reminders
Upcoming challenges or events

Once the rough draft is edited it is transferred onto a computer template for publication and distribution. It is a good link to home and gives parents information about what is going on in the school and classroom.

Rubrics We periodically use rubrics for assessing projects or presentations, performances or products. We have found that creating the rubric with the students at the onset of a project and allowing them to use it at the conclusion has been the most effective use of rubrics. If students know what the criteria are for achieving a superior level of performance they will usually aspire to it. They will also be honest in their own assessment when they know clearly what the expectations are. Students are quite good at using the rubrics for doing peer evaluation. Though there are many ready-made rubrics available in programme documents and teacher resources, we usually find ourselves using those as guides and letting the students create the wording. The following rubric is an example of what our youngest group of students came up with for assessing their presentation of a memorized poem. It is a relatively simple rubric created for the use of younger students. Other rubrics we have used involve more complex items such as level of understanding, or expression of ideas. It is not recommended to rely solely on the use of rubrics but to include a variety of assessment tools. See Blackline Master #39 for a blank rubric.

	CRITERIA	1	2	3	4
TARGET : Memorization of Poetry	**Use of voice**	can hardly hear the voice	can hear voice some of the time	loud volume clear words	plus added expression
	knowledge of poem	needed to stop & look at book 4-5 times/ made mistakes	needed to stop & look at book 2-3 times/ made mistakes	looked at book once & said the whole thing	didn't have to look at all & made no mistakes
	body movement	moved constantly not looking at audience	moved from side to side looking around	looked at audience feet still hands at side	plus uses hands for expression

Checklists have long been used by teachers as a method of data collection. There are probably as many checklists available in teacher resources as there are Harlequin Romances. The trick is finding ones that are useful and effective. They may look nice on paper, but then when you actually go to use them and evaluate the information retrieved, you find out they are more work than they are worth. We have found that checklists are useful to have next to you as you are conducting a reading, writing or math interview. It helps to focus the interview and determine what you are looking for.

What has proven to be an even more effective use of checklists has been to have checklists available to students as a self-evaluation and tracking tool. We have created checklists for student use at the writing centre, the poster project centre, the research centre, and the animal research centre. These checklists guide users through the processes that form the basis of work at these centres. They are especially helpful for project work. The checklists facilitate the stu-

Story Writing Centre

Writer: Sook-i

Title: The Day I Lost My Dog

Date: April 30, 2005

Editing Checklist

Content
- ☑ The title relates to the story.
- ☑ The introduction grabs the reader's interest.
- ☑ The conclusion makes the story complete.
- ☑ The story makes sense.
- ☑ Nothing is missing from the story.
- ☑ The story is interesting to read.

Mechanics
- ☑ The following have been checked and corrected:
- ☑ Spelling
- ☑ Capital letters
- ☑ Punctuation
- ☑ Paragraphing

Writer's Responsibility
- ☑ The writer has read this story to me.
- ☑ The writer proofread own work first, & made corrections & changes.

Editor: Oran

Story Writing Centre

Writer: Sook-i

Title: The Day I Lost My Dog

Date: April 15, 2005

Writing Process Checklist

Writing
- ☑ Your plan / web / brainstorming is complete.
- ☑ 1st rough draft is complete.
- ☑ You have read it to two editors.
- ☑ They have completed an editing checklist.
- ☑ You have revised your draft by making changes.
- ☑ You have conferenced with a teacher and made more changes.

Publishing
- ☑ You have typed it on the computer or chosen another form of publication.
- ☑ You have conferenced with a teacher again.
- ☑ You have printed out your good copy.
- ☑ You have glued your book pages.
- ☑ They have been photocopied.
- ☑ You have completed the cover and illustrations.

Date finished: May 21, 2005

dents' evaluation of their work against the listed criteria.

The added benefit of checklists is that students can follow the different processes (writing, editing, research, posters) quite independently and also can conference with each other when the requirements are clearly laid out. Consistency is maintained and the checklist forms a point of reference for anyone who gives assistance to a student. We have found them extremely useful when students follow a multi-step process. See Blackline Master #102 for blank writing checklists.

Presentation Proposal Once a publication, project, or art work is completed, students like to know that there may be other audiences available to whom they may present their work. This may be done for neighbouring classes, siblings' classrooms, the office staff, or principal. Before they do so, they are required to decide upon an appropriate audience, evaluate the required time needed for a presentation and make a request for a time and date. Once they receive a reply to a request, students make sure they keep the appontment and look forward to any feedback or constructive criticism they receive.

PRESENTATION PROPOSAL

To __Mrs. Green_____ Date __Feb. 20, 2005__

I/We would like to do a presentation of the following _____
__our country research poster on Japan_____

It would take approximately ___15___ minutes.

Could you please suggest an appropriate date and time?

Presentation date ____Feb. 21, 2005_____ Presentation time __10:00 a.m.__

Presenters __Sook-i and Fatima_____

Sign for approval _____Mrs. Green_____

Presentation proposals are also used when students wish to bring something from home (such as a special treasure or a favourite pet) to share with the whole class. On occasion we have asked students to add to the proposal an outline of the information they will present to the class related to the featured item. One of our grade four students wanted to desperately bring in his pet snake. We knew he was capable of putting together an interesting report if he was given the right parameters. His initial motivation was just to bring the snake to class and test the shock value. However, given the challenge with which we presented him, he provided the class with a complete report on the type of snake he owned, its appearance, habits, habitat, and his owner-ship, prepared in advance in a written report. He responded to some appropriate questions with sound knowledge. All in all, it was valuable learning experience for everyone. See Blackline Master # 94 for the presentation proposal form.

The **Performance Proposal** is modelled after the presentation proposal. When students indicate an interest in doing performances such as dance, drama, gymnastic routines, and music, they should have the opportunity to seek other audiences for these demonstrations as well. See the Blackline Master #94 for the performance proposal form.

·············

These are just some of the evaluation strategies and demonstrations that one could incorporate in a dynamic teaching model. Use of these strategies does not exclude the use of others, but may work in concert with other tried and true methods as long as those methods are in keeping with the basic philosophy of this child-centred, process-driven model. Evaluation practices will grow and change with you as you practise and refine your teaching methods. You are as dynamic and evolving as your students and the model you create. We too are always looking to include new technology and practices in our assessment tool kit. We often like to video tape or tape record students and their work so that they can review their performance and complete a rubric after the fact. We have recently started using the school's digital camera which downloads photos onto the computer for storage. Some of our colleagues have begun to use completely electronic portfolios, but we haven't gone that way yet. There is something to be said about the sensory gratification of paper copies which is difficult to get from a computer even if the hard copies are scanned in as exact replicas.

Whatever your choices are it is important to include a variety of methods that draw on different dimensions of the learning process. As mentioned at the beginning of this chapter it is most important that the assessment and evaluation strategies match the delivery model and actually measure what they are intended to measure. The evaluation process must take into account the interconnections of the student, teacher, curriculum and the environment.

·············

There are a number of other student demonstrations or tasks which reinforce students' learning and also provide you with information on individual abilities. We have outlined these in our next chapter entitled Daily Student Tasks

CHAPTER 10

DAILY STUDENT TASKS

Sometimes when I consider what tremendous
consequences come from little things...
I am tempted to think....
there are no little things.
—— *BRUCE BARTON*

Each day when students arrive in the morning, one of the first things they do is check the job list for the job they may have to complete. Students are given the responsibility for a variety of tasks which help maintain the class's orderliness or provide an opportunity for purposeful learning to occur. These tasks are learning enhancement activities or classroom maintenance tasks. Students have some ownership in their learning tasks and in the space in which that learning takes place.

Doing jobs for the daily class meeting

Many of the jobs are a required part of our daily class meeting. The **daily class meeting** is usually held after our morning recess break. During that time we meet with the whole group. The purpose of the meeting is to bring the group together to focus on information we may all need to share and have. We try to model our meeting on a real life meeting, where, after all preliminary reports are in, students and teachers can make new announcements, discuss upcoming events, take time to discuss any difficulties and ask for solutions and ideas. We have had some highly creative problem-solving displayed at these meetings.

The reports that children bring to this meeting are based on the job list which is displayed on a prominent front board area (as discussed in Chapter 8). These different tasks are a daily requirement and one child is responsible for one task each day. Each day we rotate the names through the list so that each child gets a turn doing the different tasks. As part of their daily job rotation, each child takes his or her turn doing the designated tasks. At our daily class meeting the child reads his/her report of the event. (The children do the job and get their report ready just after they enter in the morning, check in on the check-in board by switching their name ticket with a ticket in the required centre and then perform their job before doing their must-do centre. In that way they are prepared when the meeting is called.)

The front board has several small white message boards, a calendar, an "important message board" and an "our news" board. These provide space for recording the tasks. The front board space in the meeting area shows the importance which the teachers put on these jobs, and the clear view gives other students the opportunity to read these task reports.

Our daily job list kept growing as many ideas for the list came from the students themselves. However, when we begin each September we introduce only a portion of the jobs. This gives new students a chance to get used to things and the rest of us time to ease into the routine. It doesn't take long before we begin to add jobs, a few at a time. Usually someone from the previous year brings something up like "When can we start doing the weather report?". We make sure that a lot of modelling occurs before we hand over a job to the students when we have certain expectations in mind. This is especially necessary when we introduce a job that is brand new. However, since we are teaching in a multiage setting, we can usually rely on an "old timer" to take on a job and do some good modelling when it is something that was done the year before. You may pick and choose from our list, and even take a couple of years to implement all the jobs. Then again you may come up with your own. Following are the ones we are currently using with a brief description of each.

Learning Enhancement Tasks

Most of these jobs are incorporated into the daily class meeting. The **learning enhancement activities** come in two varieties, both of which require some method of reporting during meeting time, either writing and then presentation or just presentation. The students who are responsible for these jobs each day are to be prepared and organized in advance of the meeting (and not be scrambling around at the last minute). Most tasks can be done in five or ten minutes first thing in the morning, during activity centre time.

Our news The student on our news is free to write/record her/his own news, gather news from fellow classmates and write it on the our news board. There is always a variety of news. It can be about family members, family outings, school events, events children are part of outside of school, like baseball, soccer, and ballet. We are told of new movies children will see, dental visits, classroom visits, comments and visits from other teachers, and other members of our community. The news is as varied as our students. As this is a free writing activity, the children are encouraged to write as much as they can independently.

Quizzes of the day The student assigned to this task is responsible for writing a quiz question appropriate for the students in the class. Some students will give several questions some of which they perceive as less challenging and others as more challenging. The quizzes are usually fact-based in the areas of math, science, language, and geography. Their level of difficulty depends on the ability level of the students. When we first started having quiz of the day, we started with only one and then gradually added a quiz board for:

Math Quiz   Science Quiz
Map & Globe Quiz   Language Quiz

Our News
Today is...

Monday, March 3, 2005

Last nit I plaed a bacebal game and won. Aisha had a slepovr with Sanna. Tomoro we are going to start new centrs. Khalid's grandma is coming from Indea. Lisa is taking her cast off next weak.

by: Sarah

After the quiz segments are read, students can write answers later when other work is completed. They write these answers and their name and date on slips of paper and put them in the answer can. If their response is selected and they have the correct answer, they get to choose something from the treasure box at the end of the week. The treasure box holds a supply of little treasures such as marbles, book marks, stickers, rings, book plates, and pencils.

Math Quiz	Science Quiz	Map & Globe Quiz
How manny ways can you sho the number 100? Give egsampls. by: Khalid	What are the stages of the water cicle? by: Michael	Which continant is Lebanon in? by: Aisha

Morning message mix-up/fix-up These are actually two different but related tasks. One student writes a message to the whole class which has "mix-ups", errors made on purpose. We first saw this idea presented at a conference by Terry Johnson and saw it again subsequently in his book, *Literacy Through Literature*. It is an old idea that has been given a little life. When starting out it is a good idea to do the mix-up yourself for some time. It provides focus for some quick mini lessons. Once the student completes the message mix-up, another person finds the spelling, grammar, or other errors and rewrites or "fixes-up" the message. In the beginning it is most effective to get the whole class involved in the fix-up. Both the message mix-up and fix-up are recorded on designated white boards. Chart paper would also suffice.

Message Mix-up	Message Fix-up
Good norming, yobs and glris. Do not clean up after centre time. Put all papers in the garbig. Than do not bring anything for homeplay. by: Khalid	Good morning, boys and girls. Please clean up after centre time. Put all papers in your notebooks. Then bring unfinished work for homework. by: Sarah

Calendar The calendar set-up is loosely built around the "Math Their Way" format. For Calendar, the child is required to write the date, update the calendar by placing the date on the calendar, write the short form for the date, turn to the appropriate day of the week, record the daily tally of school days, and days of the year. The child responsible for this task reads out all this information when the teacher works through the "agenda" of the daily class meeting. See Blackline Masters #69-78 for the calendar parts.

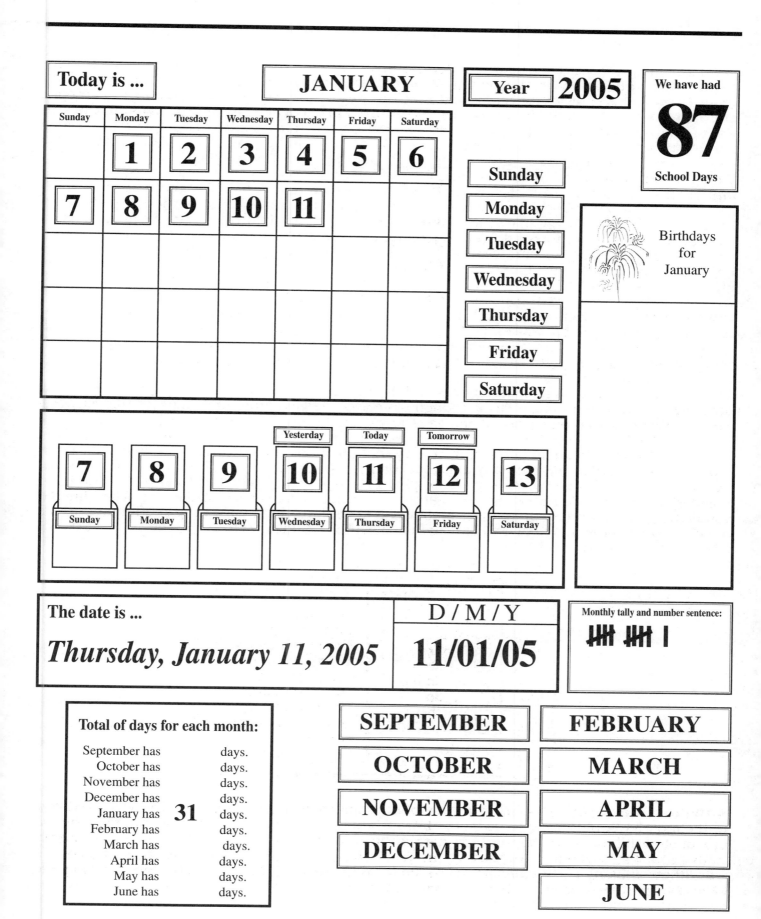

Weather graph/report For a younger group this task may simply entail graphing with pictures of the type of weather for the day. Temperature can also be recorded. At the end of each month the teachers can do tallies with the students and discuss highs and lows, types of weather etc. After several months of accumulated reports the teacher can do math related to the weather information. "How many days of rain did we have in September; in October; in November?" Older students involved in this task might be required to provide more detail than younger students in their weather reports. Students could put the thermometer outside the window, read the temperature, record it, make weather observations about wind, precipitation, types of clouds, and other weather-related facts. Students are encouraged to listen to the weather forecast on radio or TV before they come to school, so they can include as much information as possible in their weather report. A simple way for a student to bring all this information to the meeting is by cutting out the weather forecast from the morning paper. We have one student who is so conscientious, he brings the paper's weather forecast every morning just in case someone doesn't have it available. Since we have been recording the sunset and sunrise times on a graph, his efforts are appreciated!

Reminders The student responsible for this task writes any important reminders, like "remember your swimming suit for swimming class tomorrow". The reminder message is written on one of the white boards. As an alternative students have available to them blank reminder notepaper which can be posted with a magnet on the front chalkboard.

Thought for the day A student records and then explains a thought for the day such as "What goes around, comes around". These thoughts are recorded in a notebook kept for this purpose. They could be posted on cards around the room.

Poem of the day A student goes to the poetry section of the Book/Resource Centre and selects a poem to be read during the daily class meeting.

Word study In word study, ten words are chosen that share some relationship. This may be synonyms for the word 'big', ten words that end in 'ion', or the names of ten different birds. It really is open to the imagination. The audience is then challenged to name the connection for all the words. The words are recorded in a notebook kept for this purpose.

```
+---------------------------------+
|          Word Study             |
|                                 |
|   station      nation           |
|   plantation   gestation        |
|   information  relation         |
|   notion       invention        |
|   coronation                    |
|   portion                       |
+---------------------------------+
```

Announcements The student in charge of announcements is required to pay close attention to the morning's announcements on the P.A. system. Pertinent announcements are recorded on one of the white boards and read out during the meeting.

Good News! Blank certificates are provided for this task. The student responsible makes note of anyone who is working well, is helpful, or does a good deed and presents her or him with a certificate of merit during the meeting.

We present good news notes ourselves at this time to celebrate accomplishments. See Blackline Masters #100-101 for a variety of blank Good News! notes.

Good News!

Date: May 3, 2005

Geoff finished his centre this morning without taking a break and he even helped me.

from, Sanna

New word of the day A new or unusual word is chosen from the dictionary and its definition is read to the class during meeting. Then the word is written on a card and posted on the wall to build a word bank.

Joke of the day We have an assortment of joke books from which a joke or riddle is chosen and read to the class. Then someone from the audience attempts to supply the answer or punch line.

Newspaper report The person responsible for this task brings an article of interest from the daily newspaper and reads it to the class. The article is kept in a folder for future reference.

Book talk This job is posted after we have taught students how to present a book talk during a language lesson and everyone has done at least one so that the students have a frame of reference. (A book talk report is done orally and requires no writing. The student has to pick a book which has been read and is a favourite. It is then presented to the class in the form of a book talk.) See Blackline Masters #108-109 for blank book talk forms.

Chairperson After several months we hand over this job to a student. The chairperson conducts the meeting, calls on presenters, keeps it on track, and also evaluates how well it went.

Timekeeper Because time can really be gobbled up during the meeting (as happens in many business meetings!) we try to make the students aware of being as efficient as possible and staying on track. At the end of the meeting the timekeeper records the total time taken and compares it to the previous day. This data could also be recorded on a graph.

Conducting the daily class meeting

All the learning enhancement tasks are given a forum at the class meeting. At the beginning of the year, we model these tasks for a few weeks. Students take on these tasks as soon as they understand how to do them, how to record, and how to report the information. To begin the class meeting, everyone is called to order by the chairperson and the timekeeper starts the clock. It usually takes about ten to twelve minutes although our record may be six minutes. The presenters are usually called upon in the same order each day. We start with the calendar, then the quizzes and message mix-up/fix-up, then the poem, thought, word, joke of the day, then the weather and newspaper reports, and finish off with our news and Good News! If we have other business to add to the meeting, we post an agenda on the board and address the items when the regular business is completed.

Maintenance Tasks

Attendance The student responsible for attendance goes to the check-in board, removes any name tickets that remain in their name pockets. This student then does a double check to see if that student is present or merely forgot to switch the tickets. The remaining name tickets are brought to the teacher who then can record the absent students on the office attendance card. The attendance job person also records the names of those absent on a designated spot on our important message board at the front. Most schools, including ours, require this list be brought to the office for follow-up and the person on attendance takes it.

Tidy Inspector The tidy inspector is required to do a thorough inspection of the room at the beginning of the daily class meeting which follows activity time. This person can remind others to replace their possessions to designated spots, help tidy, and put unclaimed items in the class lost and found bin. The inspector can reward a group or individuals if their space is very tidy with a tidy inspector award during the class meeting. We also have champion classroom cleaner certificates. A list of criteria for keeping the classroom clean is posted in the classroom. See Blackline Master #105 for the awards.

Filer This person is responsible for returning all teacher-marked work from the "work to be filed bucket" to the group or book buckets. If some work samples are marked **P** for portfolio they are put into the portfolio file box for filing later. If marked with **WW**, the work is posted on the writers' wall.

Mail sorter This student has to place all letters and notices from the class and/or office in the students' mail boxes. These are usually kept in a mail basket next to the mail boxes until the mail sorter completes the job.

Ticket inspector Everyone is supposed to return their own tickets at the end of activity time but sometimes this doesn't happen. This inspector checks to see that all name tickets and centre tickets have been returned to the right pocket.

Recycle bin On student is responsible for taking out the recycle bins to the main collection area at any free moment in the day.

Floor The floor inspector makes sure errant items of paper and garbage are removed from the floor when necessary during the day.

Tables This job requires the student to inspect tables to ensure that classmates have returned all materials to their proper place. It is especially helpful after activity centre time.

Chairs It is the student on chairs duty to make sure that they are put away and pushed in throughout the day to avoid any unnecessary bumps and bruises.

Bookshelves Our classroom books are always in need of sorting and reshelving for maximum daily efficiency. Any books that have been borrowed from the school library are picked up from the "library book return bucket" and delivered to the library by this person.

In the Hallway We usually have two students take this job on at once. These students are responsible for checking on the tidiness of the hallway as students have coat hooks and a rack in a recessed area outside of the classroom. These student monitors also have first dibs on working or reading in the hallway (a cherished privilege) when the opportunity arises.

Ball outside Each year we usually have at least one ball that someone can take outside to play with during outdoor recess. Putting it on a job arrow eliminates the hassle of someone missing out. This year we have been given a number of balls and outdoor equipment (Frisbee, skipping ropes, etc.) which are kept in a very large Rubbermaid™ bin. An inventory list is kept on the outside of the bin and it is this student's job to check that all items are returned after recesses.

Washer Our class eats lunch in the classroom at their group tables. This person wipes down each table after lunch.

Dryer This person follows the washer, and dries off the lunch tables.

Water plants We have a number of plants in the science area which require monitoring and watering.

These jobs, as you can see, greatly relieve the teacher of the many little tasks required to keep everything running smoothly. Our aim is to have students have ownership of the classroom and the materials. In this way they are more likely to take better care of everything.

....

The real life tasks incorporated into our classroom help develop numeracy and literacy skills, while making learning meaningful. The students have responsibility and ownership of these tasks and are happy and excited when they have their turn. They feel important as they have to make decisions on what to record and report. Children begin to make links with their school work and real life when given the opportunity to take on real tasks and responsibilities in the daily routine and running of our classroom.

CHAPTER 11

SCHEDULING

We work not only to produce
but to give value to time.
— EUGENE DELACROIX

What does time mean in a dynamic classroom?

Time is of the essence in everyone's lives and no more so than in the dynamic classroom. The traditional classroom is often governed by discrete units of time, controlled by a timetable, clock, and ringing bells, with the necessity to change subjects as the periods change. The dynamic classroom requires large blocks of work time and fluidity and flexibility in its scheduling.

Since the dynamic classroom is process-oriented as opposed to solely product-oriented, students often interconnect a variety of skills while completing a research project, designing a poster, writing a letter, or publishing a book. Making large blocks of time available becomes both necessary and desirable. (In this type of classroom set-up there is never a fear that perhaps if things are not timed properly, the one student who manages to whiz through his seat work will not have something to do.) Students regularly engage in projects over several days, seeing the process through from beginning to end. Time is not the governing factor, but rather a reality with which students contend and use to the best of their ability.

Frequently, students request extra work time during recesses or lunch hours, which they then use to complete a project. They are motivated to use every bit of time made available to them. If time is left after completing a required math assignment for example, students are self-directed enough to proceed to work on projects in progress. Organizational systems are in place which allow students to access independently the materials needed to continue working on projects from day to day. The students' independence means it is no more work for us as teachers to have several different learning activities being underway.

Because the dynamic classroom functions most successfully with an integrated curriculum, it can be difficult for an outside observer to identify the blocks of time normally seen in a traditional classroom for different curriculum strands. In a dynamic classroom these strands are interwoven into the fabric of the day. During morning activity centre time, most core curriculum subjects are being studied concurrently by different groups of children. Some group

Monday, May 3, 2005 document

Monday, May 3, 2005

8:30 a.m. Activity Centres

Students in their groups go to the group must-do centres.

recess

10:10-10:20 a.m. Class Meeting
10:20-11:30 a.m. Math/Science/Technology

One of these subjects is blocked in for this period. The whole class receives a lesson and then works on using new information, either in groups, with a partner or individually.

12:30-1:10 p.m. Frenc

1:10-1:50 p.m. Comp

Group B - Language Les

2:05-2:50 p.m. Sharin

Reminders: *Staff Meeti*

Weekly timetable

Time	Monday	Tuesday	Wednesday	Thursday	Friday
8:30-9:55	Activity Centres				Assembly / Language Session
9:55-10:10	recess				
10:10-11:30	Math/Science/Technology				The Writing Process
11:30-12:30	lunch				
12:30-1:10	French				
1:10-1:50	Group A Computer Lab Group B Language	Phys. Ed.	Phys. Ed.	Group B Computer Lab Group A Language	Portfolio Session
1:50-2:05	recess				
2:05-2:50	Sharing QRT Reading Response	QRT Reading Response	Sharing QRT Reading Response	Phys. Ed.	Sharing QRT Reading Response
2:50-3:00	clean-up and home time				

lessons can be presented if the need arises.

Following the morning activity time, the daily class meeting takes place. The remainder of the morning is used to teach. The focus of our teaching is the provision of specific information necessary for children to engage in centre activities. We often call this "teaching to a centre". Since large blocks of time are still necessary for this type of teaching, topics may alternate from day to day. We strive to equip the children with the necessary tools for independent centre work. With such teaching and guidance, they become better able to be self-directed, make choices relevant to them, and achieve a higher degree of success. The rest of the day's time is flexible and scheduled according to the specific needs of the students. Our day includes an independent reading time, a time for shared reading or reading to children, reflective journal writing, and catch-up work time.

Time takes on a different meaning not only throughout the day in a dynamic classroom, but throughout the year. Units of study require several months to complete. For instance, as our class explores the environment and our responsibility to it, students will have the opportunity to develop this theme over six months through a variety of centres and subtopics. Because students are given time to practise many processes of learning in a variety of formats, skills are honed and information banks are filled. Learning has a better chance at being interconnected and refined when units of study are integrated. Transference is also more likely to occur.

It is a difficult task for a teacher to schedule for all that is required in a day. If students are allowed to have some input as to how their time will be utilized, they are more likely to remain committed to their tasks. Students learn how to make use of every unit of time available, a skill many adults have yet to master. We use daily class meeting time to elicit input from students regarding the schedule and whenever possible incorporate suggestions.

A sample schedule

In our class, the basic framework of our schedule is maintained but is tailored to the particular day's needs each morning. The day's schedule is posted on a white board for students to view first thing when they enter. As long as they know what is ahead in any given day they are satisfied and can comfortably work within changes. Once they recognize its value they really count on seeing a complete schedule displayed when they come in. We have included a weekly schedule and a sample day book page with a detailed description of our daily routine. See Blackline Masters #14-15 for blank schedule and day book pages.

Our daily routine is as follows:

8:30   The bell rings
· students arrive.
· each student takes his/her own name card from its pocket and places it in a box before sitting on their place on the carpet.
(This is the routine for the "training period". Once routines are established the students will go to their assigned jobs and centres using the check-in system as soon as they come in after the bell.)
· students check "job list" to determine the jobs for the day.
· students get on with assigned tasks such as attendance, etc.
· others should be settled on the carpet for when morning announcements begin.
(For the first weeks we teach and model how to do the calendar, date, weather, morning message, our news, and quizzes of the day, and review the requirements at centres.)

8:55   Centres
· name cards are handed out in random order.
· students choose their centre ticket and go to their centre.
(During the first week or so, the students are exploring the centres

according to their own interests using the check-in system board. Once they have become sufficiently familiar with the way things operate, they are assigned one must-do centre per day, on a rotating basis.)
- when the activity requirements are completed students sign off their work log before going on to another centre.
- hand things into the "finished work buckets".
- tidy centre before vacating it.
- if time allows another centre may be chosen by changing the ticket.

9:50   Tidy-up time
- everyone contributes to the clean-up until the entire room is tidy.
(As most things have a label and/or a specific location for storage, it is expected that the children return all materials to their assigned locations.)
- work is dated or date stamped before it is handed in.
- work that is to be taken home is put in mailboxes or saved for portfolios.
- unfinished writing goes into the individual writing folders for completion later.

9:55   Recess

10:10   Snack time
- students have a snack break at their group tables.
(In two schools we have worked, a scheduled snack time was used to reduce the amount of garbage left outdoors. However, last year we decided to give our students a choice as to when they would have a snack break in the morning. They each have brought a place mat from home so when they have completed their must-do centre they can take a snack break before going onto something else. They find a vacant table and use their place mat to keep things tidy. We have found this approach saves time. It also serves to motivate students to get work done so they can join their friends in a snack break.)

10:20   Daily class meeting time
- the whole class sits together on the carpet for meeting.
- students present their learning enhancement tasks.
- the teacher presents any relevant information for the day or week.
(Details of the daily class meeting's structure are discussed in Chapter 10.)

10:35   Mathematics
- lessons and activities take place during this time slot.
(It can also be integrated with language and environmental studies lessons.)

Environmental Studies/Science
- experiments, science logs, reading and writing, can all be part of this learning time. (Math and science can be alternated each day to make use of larger blocks of time.)

11:30   Lunch

12:30   French

1:10   Gym, Library, Computer Lab or Music
(These are scheduled in by the school administration.)

1:50   Recess

2:05   Language Lesson
· a variety of lessons are presented here, depending on the needs of students: from process writing, play writing, spelling, grammar, letter writing, reading for a purpose, analyzing and studying a story, etc.

Quiet reading time (QRT)
· students pick 3 books and find a quiet spot in the room to remain for the whole quiet reading time.
· no more than 2 people can share one space.
· a countdown to "freeze" is called, after which no one is to leave their reading spot.
· books may be exchanged with a reading partner but no one is to get up and get another book from the shelf at this time.
· the teacher may want to conduct reading interviews during this time.

Story time
· whole group shared reading or guided reading on the carpet.

Sharing time
· one group shares some of their work done during centre time, according to a sign up list on the board.
· the audience asks questions and makes comments at the end.
· a teacher or a student records an entry in the "sharing book". This is read with the whole class and often revisited by individuals during quiet reading time. (The sharing book is a blank spiral bound book to record observations, comments, and the topics of each presentation.)

3:00   Dismissal

....

It is difficult for any teacher to apply this schedule exactly to a specific class. Schools have particular scheduling limitations which change from year to year. Although we are usually required to change our schedule each school year, we always try to remain true to its basic framework. After experimenting with other scheduling approaches we have found that this framework functions best for us.

....

Once you have your schedule in place you are ready to move on. We'll offer you some tips and hints about getting started in the year which we've learned by trial and error but personal experience and your own instincts will be your best guide.

CHAPTER 12

GETTING STARTED IN THE YEAR

Whatever you can do, or dream you can,
do it. Boldness has genius,
power and magic in it.
— GOETHE

Now we have the dreams and tools to move beyond words and history,
beyond the possible to the imagined, and into life both ancient and new,
where we will look back to see our present dreams
trailing behind us as markers of where we have been.
— GLORIA STEINEM

September has arrived. You have worked hard to get your classroom and the necessary materials organized. The space and the location of the permanent centres have been planned. All buckets, bins, and shelves are labelled. The pocket charts for the check-in system have been constructed. Materials and task cards are ready for the centres. Your evaluation binders are organized, and you have prepared a portfolio for each student. You have planned hard and now you are ready for your students. The checklist on the following page will help you assure yourself that you are ready to face your students on the first day of school.

We have found that if we consciously set aside approximately the first month as a training period, we are able to ease both students and teachers new to this model into their roles. This provides all participants with enough time to become familiar and comfortable with the systems and routines

The training period

How are all the components of the dynamic teaching model introduced to the students? We recommend that the first three weeks to a month of school be considered a training period

The Dynamic Teaching Model Checklist

❏ Have you chosen the outcomes and related centres?
❏ Have you designed the classroom space to facilitate the centres?
❏ Have you set aside a meeting area?
❏ Have you set up your student groups?
❏ Have you labelled your materials and their location?
❏ Have you set up a place for your must-do list?
❏ Have you set up a class list with the job list?
❏ Have you made your writer's wall?
❏ Have you made the art gallery?
❏ Do you have a work log for each student?
❏ Do you have your notebooks and book buckets ready?
❏ Do you have your evaluation/recording binders organized?
❏ Do you have student portfolios made for each student?
❏ Do you have a mailbox for each student?
❏ Do you have recording sheets prepared for the centres?
❏ Do you have a schedule that has large blocks of time?

for your students. Now is the most important time of the year to introduce how the systems all work together so as to make a very organized classroom. However, please take things slowly. The time you invest now, training the students, will result in a smoothly running programme.

For this training period we do not use a theme, or at least not a theme in its purest form. Our focus is on learning and practising the systems of the dynamic teaching model. We use open-ended and familiar concepts and skills to facilitate students in becoming accustomed to doing centre activities. During the remainder of the year, the tasks that are at the centres are loosely organized around a topic of study. This topic is applied to centre activities only where they naturally fit. Other centres stand alone and always rely on student choices for focus. Some of the theme-fitting centres are topic-related and the direct teaching periods also relate to this topic. We schedule specific lessons to provide background information related to the topic. We also provide children opportunities to do investigations related to the topic. Children have a lot to learn during the training period: all the components of the dynamic classroom, and organizational processes. Therefore, we allow for more free exploration, while introducing a variety of topics and activities so children get used to what is expected of them. This allows children time to practice skills they have forgotten over the summer, revisit those skills with which they feel comfortable and gain the confidence to tackle new ideas of their own. Begin the month knowing that you will focus on process as opposed to product.

Teaching how to use activity centres

The students are not going to innately know what the expectations for doing centres are. During this training period the time you put into explaining the specific expectations for working at centres will pay off in the long run. Here are our suggestions for getting started.

• Decide which centres you want opened first. We suggest that you open those that are the easier ones to maintain, and the easier ones for the children to work through. Let's look at one sample classroom. You have thirty students, and six children in each of five groups. Given that each group will spend one activity period per day at one centre, you will need to organize five must-do centres for the students to work through in a five day period. You will also need to have other centres open so students have a choice of activities once they have finished their required centre and before activity time is over.

- To get the students used to the idea of how centres work and how to use the check-in system, gather the students together in the meeting area. Show the children the pockets with their names.
- Call out names randomly from the pile of name tickets they have handed in when first entering the classroom and get each child to place their name card in their own pocket. After everyone has their name ticket in the name pocket explain that this is where they will find their name card each morning.
- Introduce the pocket charts with the centre logos on each pocket. Explain that the children will find tickets in the centres that are open. The most important rule is:

You must have a ticket in order to go to a centre.

- Go to the front board where you have placed the group symbols and point out with the students, the designated must-do centre for each group. For example, the red circles must-do the blocks centre, the blue diamonds must do the puzzles centre and the Orange Rectangles must do the math centre, and so on.
- Demonstrate how to find the centre in the pocket chart, select a ticket to allow entry and to place it in your name pocket. You then move the name ticket in that centre pocket. Then get a few children to demonstrate.
- Before allowing the children to go and start their centres, you still need to explain where things are and how to treat them, and how they need to put things away exactly where they are found. Stress the double labelling system and how the students will have to be inspectors to ensure that everything is put carefully away.
- Explain that signs are posted to help find the materials and location of centres around the classroom. You may wish to walk about the classroom, pointing out the various locations of things.
- Then allow the children to go group by group to the check-in board, select their centre ticket and switch centre tickets with the name tickets and go to the designated centre.

The main idea for this practising period is to introduce the different elements of the system slowly. Students need to practise what is expected, and to have the opportunity to clarify any questions they have regarding work or behaviour. Going slowly gives the teacher time to see what is the next thing that the children are ready to take on. To provide ample time for clarification, introductions, and demonstrations, we bring the whole group together at our meeting place both at the beginning and at the end of activity time, during the first month. Once children have the routines down, they enjoy being allowed to immediately get to their must-do as soon as they check in.

Take it one step at a time

Teachers are tempted to introduce all the components of all the organizational systems over a shorter space of time. Please resisit this urge. Your patience in going slowly will pay off handsomely later in the year when you notice how smoothly things are going. Pacing in this training month is key to preparing your students to be independent, cooperative, collaborative learners. As mentioned in Chapter 8: Classroom Management and Organization, we have created a set of posters which outline some of the routines and learning processes, such as behaviour during the meeting, keeping the classroom clean, etc. (See Blackline Masters #42-52.) One way we pace ourselves is by introducing a couple of these organizational strategies per day along with centres.

For example, on the first day you would introduce how the check-in system works. You would have each child do their must-do. Then ensure you have enough time to do a clean up and inspection of the room and its resources. This is when you might go over the poster on keeping the classroom clean. On the second day, you might choose a centre or two to introduce and discuss in detail the specific expectations of each before allowing the children to get going with their must-do centre. You may model some learning behaviours you wish to see. You may introduce the idea that each student will record her/his work, draw a diagram and/or write a report for each must-do centre. You may or may not actually require the students to do this until the second or third week of activity centres, depending on the group with which you are working.

Each day, introduce a few more centres, giving thorough explanations of the what, why and how of each one. It will be necessary to show the children where they store their notebooks and other log books. They will need to know where to place completed assignments to be marked as soon as you require them to record their work, or do a report. You may wish to discuss what is appropriate for a report, or you may have students share some exemplary work, so as to demonstrate to others how to work. Encourage the groups to help each other when they have queries or meet difficulties with their expected tasks.

Next, introduce the idea of the work log. Explain how to record required tasks each day. To begin you can have the whole group assembled, pass out the work logs, show them how to list the must-do activity, and the centre. Indicate where on the form the student checks off if he/she has completed the task, and assigns a number value for how well he/she has done. (As mentioned in Chapter 9: Evaluation and Authentic Assessment, the values are outlined on the level of performance poster.) On the day you introduce how this is used, make sure you give extra time towards the end of activity time to allow students to complete the sheet. It may be necessary to give students frequent reminders to complete their work log entry. Also allow time to check with students for feedback and queries.

Insist the students tidy up at the end of activity time during this training session. At the end of each activity time, comment on the behaviours you really liked and then ask a few children to voice what they saw which they liked. Children become very good at noting good working behaviours.

After each group has done the required activity centres for the cycle, you may notice that some children have some work or reports unfinished. During the training period catch-up days are scheduled once students have been to three or fours centres and there is a need to have a little extra catch-up time. On these days movement to the next must-do centre is suspended. Catch-up days allow children an additional activity time to complete any unfinished activity tasks. On catch-up days students refer to their work logs to note which centres remain unfinished. We check work logs weekly against our must-do centre tracking binder. On the work log under the column "checked" we mark "√" when an activity is finished and "•" when an activity requires further work. Their goal is to be checked off by the teacher at the end of each week. Then the student gets "signed off" and is able to make a free choice at any activity centre that is open. Free choice is a motivational force for many students to finish work each day. If students complete all tasks for a week they receive a small Good News! certificate of recognition.

Once you have completed one cycle which includes a catch-up day then you will see how you need to adjust the pace for your group. Remember, you are designing your own dynamic classroom based on the needs of your students. You may need to schedule two catch-up days in the cycle. You may decide that as you develop more sophisticated, complex, or detailed tasks, you want the students to use two days at each centre before moving on to the next centre. In this way you eliminate the need for a catch-up day. Often, this provides a better work rhythm for older students who want to pursue larger and more in-depth projects. In Chapter 13: Up and Running, we discuss alternative methods to scheduling whole catch-up days.

There are timetable slots later in the day which are usually allotted for the teaching of topic-related material. However, during the training month, we use this time for instructions and explanations of routines and centre design. We often use the time to introduce specific required tasks of a centre. The use of this time is flexible. For example we may address particular centres, record or report student tasks, demonstrate how to select items to display on the writer's wall, or introduce and model the steps in the writing process. Flexibility is the key. As a teacher you can best appraise the particular needs of the students you have, and decide on what should be further explained.

During the first month, we also use the daily class meeting time to train the students for all the tasks that have to be done at the beginning of the activity centre time, which are reported by the designated students during our daily class meeting. This is in Chapter 10: Daily Student Tasks. After you have expanded on the tasks from the job list, allow children during activity centre time to record their task before before they begin their must-do centre. We set a time limit by which all jobs are to be completed and when students should be at work on their must-do centres.

In planning the second round or cycle of must-do centres, think about what other centres could be introduced, what ones should be kept, and if different task cards need to be developed for them. During the third cycle we allow for more independent practice, and do fine tuning and make adjustments. As more children will be independent you can spend time with those who will require individual attention to learn how to complete the expected tasks.

Three cycles of the training period

A sample time line of three cycles of centres during the training period follows. This is not an exact recipe. We make adjustments each year to suit the needs of the students. You may need to slow down or speed up. You decide. Take your lead from the children.

First Cycle: Introductions
Duration: 6 days
Day 1
· meet with the whole group.
· introduce check-in system.
· show location of materials, and centres.
· introduce the work log recording system.
· allow students to try the available centres.
· allow feedback session at close.
Day 2
· introduce a centre or two in detail.
· practice check-in system.
· choose an available centre.
· record in work log.
· allow feedback session.
Day 3
· introduce another centre or two in detail.
· practice check-in system.
· introduce the must-do centres.
· record in work log.
· allow feedback session.
Day 4
· introduce idea of reporting and recording after each must-do.
· show children where and how to report.
· introduce where group buckets are located so they can get their notebooks for their recording.
· indicate where to put work to get it marked by the teacher.
· practise check-in system.
· begin must-do centres.
· allow for feedback.

Day 5
· continue to introduce new centres.
· practise check-in.
· do must-do's.
· write a report/record work in notebooks.
· submit work to be marked.
· allow for feedback.
· teacher checks work logs to prepare for catch-up day.
Day 6
· introduce catch-up day/free choice.
· complete unfinished work and provide feedback.

Cycle Two: Coaching
Duration: 6 or 7 days
· meet with the whole group.
· introduce the marking of work logs and cross tracking by teacher.
· continue to introduce the procedures and expectations of new centres, their tasks and the use and care of materials. This can be done later in the day. As necessary, review previously introduced routines and their rationale.
· continue to model, demonstrate reports, and recording of tasks.
· introduce our writer's wall.
· review catch-up and free choice days.
· prepare students for the next round of centres they will be expected to practise on their own.

Cycle Three: Independent Practice
Duration: 6 or 7 days
· allow students to do the check-in immediately upon entering.
· check the job list before going to must-do centre.
· students may need some reminders; complete task report, complete work logs, put away materials, place completed work in bin to be marked, etc.
· introduce idea of portfolios and discuss how and why work is placed there.
· provide feedback session at end of round.

This time line is a sample of what the training period could look like. Please do not consider this a hard and fast schedule to follow as it is provided as a guide only. In the training period, the emphasis is on taking things at a pace slow enough to provide children time to practise new procedures, to adjust to new expectations, and to clarify information. You can also fine tune the procedures as you and your class discuss them during the feedback sessions. Remember to elicit ideas regarding procedures and organization from the students. We have found that they often provide innovative and creative ideas on how to run things. This also provides students with a sense of ownership and pride in their class. They know that what they think is valued when their ideas are adopted for general use.

Often when we have what we consider to be several good ideas on how to solve an organizational or procedural problem that affects the whole class, we discuss the pros and cons of them with the students and take a class vote to decide on the favoured approach.

············

By slowly and deliberately building the organizational components of an active classroom, you are laying a solid foundation on which to build a structure that will be both strong, functional, and pleasing. Once the necessary routines are known and expectations are understood, you can move out of the training period mode and into keeping the programme running.

CHAPTER 13

UP AND RUNNING

While one person hesitates because he feels inferior,
the other is busy making mistakes
and becoming superior.
— HENRY C. LINK

The secret of joy in work is contained in one word — excellence.
To know how to do something well is to enjoy it.
— PEARL S. BUCK

Maintaining the model

Now the programme is up and running. You and your students may still feel a little over-whelmed, but a month's worth of practice will hopefully have increased your comfort level. You know where you need to increase the demands of certain tasks. You can see the children have been very pleased with the success of their accomplishments. They are eager to share their work. They have understood the routines and need fewer and fewer reminders. Things are pro-gressing.

Your efforts will be on maintaining the programme. If you teach thematically, you may now like to begin with several rounds of centres that are focussed on a particular theme. You and your students may have chosen a theme or you may have to follow those chosen in your school or provincial/state curriculum guidelines. By now you will see a need to schedule in catch-up times for students to allow time with certain centres. You can clearly see the progress being made on the student work logs.

Scheduling in catch-up and free choice times

It won't be long after the training period to see a need to schedule some catch-up time in different ways than you did in the training period. We use two methods. As mentioned in the previous chapter, one way we schedule catch-up time is by setting catch-up days for the whole class. This means no one group proceeds to the next centre. All students take note of what activities are not finished and work to catch up. The bonus for students who are all up-to-date is that they get free choice. It is best to use catch-up time in this way for a few cycles so you can monitor how students are handling catch-up time and reinforce proper procedures. Catch-up time may work best this way for as long as the first two or three months.

Once everyone understands the value of making the best use of catch-up time (meaning no centre homework and the opportunity for free choice) we add catch-up cards and free choice cards to the line up of must-do centres on the front board. You will need to have catch-up tickets available in the pocket of the check-in system. You will only have one or two groups on catch-up to follow, while everyone else is at their must-do centre. When using this method students put their name cards in a catch-up pocket on the check-in system's planning board and take a pink catch-up card to put in their name pocket. It is easy to tell who is doing what with a glance at the planning board. You can play with the order of your catch-up cards and the number of them. We also add a free choice card to the line up to give everyone something to look forward to. The bottom line is that the individual students must be all caught up with their must-do centres before taking a free choice centre even if their group has landed on free choice.

Must-do Centres:

Groups:

Groups move one space per day in this direction.

In option 1 only those people who are up to date will be able to have free choice and it is likely that some people will never get there.

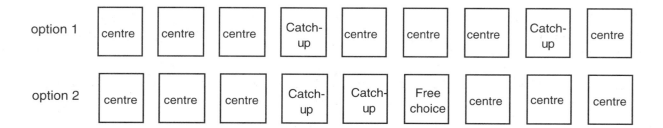

In option 2 everyone has a greater chance of getting a free choice option because you have given them two days in a row to do some catching up. The motivation is possibly stronger since they are not as likely to give up with the feeling that free choice is impossible to attain. It is not long before students recognize the rewards of staying up to date. By now more of the centres are open so there is a greater variety of activities from which to choose.

Creating and maintaining the centres

One of your jobs will be to develop task cards for centres. We usually plan ahead by listing the next cycle of centres we want to prepare on a must-do list, such as on the following. We

Must-do Planning List		
Period beginning: 29 09 05	Period ending: 24 10 05	
Centre:	**Activity:**	**Expectations:**
art centre	silhouette	understand symmetry
math centre	calculations	use 3 digit numbers
Map&globe	continents	learn parts of the world

Centres for the Year

- *animal research*
- *art*
- *banking/money*
- *big books*
- *board games*
- *book/resource*
- *calculator*
- *calendar*
- *Canadiana*
- *construction*
- *consumer affairs*
- *correspondence*
- *cursive writing*
- *dance*
- *design a solution*
- *drama*
- *drawing*
- *ecology*
- *experiments*
- *grammar examiner*
- *history*
- *inventions*
- *journal writing*
- *make-a-book*
- *map and globe*
- *math blocks*
- *math games*
- *math problems*
- *measurement*
- *media*
  - *audio*
  - *film projector*
  - *overhead projector*
  - *video*
- *music*
- *newspaper*
- *novel study*
- *paint easel*
- *personal well-being*
- *poetry study*
- *poster projects*
- *publishing centre*
- *puzzles*
- *research projects*
- *science*
- *sculpture*
- *shared reading*
- *spelling*
- *story study*
- *story writing*
- *technology tools*
- *weather*

found that by looking ahead to the next set of centres we could develop task cards that introduced a new skill, or concept for the next few cycles. Instead of just preparing one or two task cards for a centre we would push ourselves to do five or six task cards so that centre would be ready for several cycles. (See Blackline Master #8 for a blank must-do planning list.)

There are many different types of tasks that may be available at centres. We have designed two major types of tasks. One type is a task card that usually has activities categorized in three challenge levels. Level 1 is the easiest while Level 3 is the most challenging. The students can choose to begin at Level 1 and work through to Level 3 or simply complete one level. You may choose to set the expectations for completion. The second type of task is open-ended. The expectation in open-ended tasks is that students work at optimal level of ability to achieve success. The instructions for these open-ended tasks come in the form of a task card, and/or may include a report or a response sheet.

The following are samples of the types of tasks provided at centres. The newspaper centre's "Newspaper Navigation #1" is a sample of a task card written in three challenge levels. When we developed this activity, we also wrote "Newspaper Navigation #2, 3, & 4" task cards to build on the concepts and skills of #1.

Newspaper Centre:
Newspaper Navigation #1

Use the newspapers to answer the following questions in your Everything Book. (You may work at the level that is most challenging for you.

Level 1	Level 2	Level 3
1. Name three parts of the newspaper.	1. Name three parts of the newspaper and describe what they are about.	1. Read one article and give a summary of it.
2. Record the date for the newspaper and how much it costs.	2. Find a headline about Canadian news and record it.	2. Name the different types of information found in a newspaper.
3. Write out two headlines.	3. Make up two headlines for our school news.	3. Describe how a newspaper is different from a book. You may use a chart.

From the animal research centre, we have an example of an open-ended task card.

Animal Research Centre:
Animals in Your Community

Investigate some of the animals that make their home in your community.

Choose six animals and draw a diagram for each and colour them.

Label the diagrams and then record facts about the animals under the pictures in the boxes.

Glue your work into your Science Log.

1.	2.
3.	4.
5.	6.

While the requirements may appear simple at first glance, students will respond in varying degrees of detail depending on their levels of ability and interest. The materials and direction for research are provided by the teacher. The teacher determines the scope of the task.

Our third sample is from the book/resource centre. It is an example of an open-ended task in a response sheet format.

Book/Resource Centre

The Book Response

Story book title: _____

Author: _____

What happens in the story?

_____

_____

_____

My favourite character in the story is _____

_____

because _____

_____

Read by: _____

The best part of the story is when _____

_____

_____

_____

_____

The illustrations are _____

_____

Three reasons I would recommend this story:

1. _____

2. _____

3. _____

Some centres such as those mentioned in the samples above need to be prepared in advance. For longer shelf life, we mount the task cards on card stock and laminate them. The reports and response sheets are kept either in Ziploc® bags or pocket folders. We have built up our task cards, and activities over a number of years. Because they are applicable to a variety of ages and abilities we see our accumulation of resources are used from year to year. As time goes on, there is less need to create new centre materials.

Some centres are not as labour intensive to create and maintain as others. For example, at the writing centre the main goal is for students to practise the writing process. To accomplish this, students have available rough draft writing booklets, editing checklists, writing webs, dictionaries, thesauruses, story starter ideas on cards, and writing utensils. The only requirement for maintenance at this type of centre is that supplies be replenished. Parent volunteers are great in helping to replenish the dwindling stocks in centres. They can be very helpful in making booklets, copying report forms, cutting art paper and poster paper, etc.

When making selections for the next cycle of centres, it is important that you consider balancing the strands of the core curriculum and the outcomes you desire. For the sake of the teacher's workload, offset labour-intensive with easier-to-maintain centres. If you choose your centres for the next cycle while students are working on the current ones, you can design the tasks and prepare materials well ahead of time and avoid a last minute rush. This is our preferred mode of operation.

Since we have been working at designing learning centre activities for a number of years now, we have accumulated a storehouse of materials. These will be available as companion publications in the near future.

Introducing new centres in the next cycle

Take the time before beginning a new cycle of centres to introduce each must-do centre or you will be inundated with questions when the children attempt to do them. We usually have an afternoon meeting or two on the days immediately before we begin the next round of centres. The task cards, additional materials and report forms, if required, are stored in a bin labelled with the centre graphic. We show the children what is in each bin, and tell them what work is required, and where to locate information. Some centres will require specific teaching. These are lessons we plan for and schedule in before new centres start. Planning for the next cycle of centres should begin well before the end of your current one.

When we have specific lessons to teach for specific centres, we schedule those centres later on in our line up of the must-do centres, giving ourselves more time to teach to that centre. Prior to the introduction of a new cycle of centres, we use direct teaching lesson time, to teach the lessons for the specific centres. We use our language lesson slots to cover centre lessons related to language (ie. spelling, grammar, writing process). Our science/math lesson time can be used to provide particular information on the science or environmental studies topic, the "how to" of an experiment, or the design of a problem solving model.

Later in the year this flow of lessons, new centre, lessons, new centre will be as natural as water flowing down a stream. There will be skills and approaches revisited in new centres (perhaps in a slightly different way) so you won't always be teaching from scratch. When that starts happening you can schedule smaller chunks of time to introduce new centres. We use part of our morning centre time, perhaps for two mornings in a row, to introduce the new centres on the same day that the students are going to start them. The introductions are made and off the students go to their first new centre while everything is fresh in their minds.

You may come up with another way of scheduling all of this which makes better sense to you. There is always room for change in the dynamic teaching model.

Posting unfinished work lists

Once you are into must-do centre work that features your required curriculum, it is vital that students complete as much of their work as possible. We have found that posting the names of students on a list of must-do centres, gives students another way to see what they still need to do. We usually encourage students to take unfinished work home for homework. We will provide photocopies of activity centre cards which we keep in our upright file box organized by centre for this purpose. Students happily cross their name off the list when they have completed something for homework.

UNFINISHED WORK AS OF APRIL 21				
ART CENTRE •birds•	MATH CENTRE •add•	SCIENCE CENTRE •energy•	POETRY CENTRE •acrostic•	DRAMA CENTRE •puppets•
Kathy	Yusef	Khalid	Mikos	Lisa
Aisha	Matt	Dawn	Pawel	Sara
Omar	Oaul	Helga	Kathy	Rona
Sook-i	Oran	Sanna	Omar	Jenn
	Fatima	Glen	Darren	Brian
		Pawel		Kyle
		Emma		Marc
				Omar
				Helga

Using project/interview days

Once procedures are under way, and students are well into the projects, we usually see a need to allow for some larger chunks of time dedicated to project work. We then designate a few days as project/interview days. We use this time to schedule reading, writing and math interviews while most students are engaged with their projects. We find this particularly helpful when report card time is coming up. We set guidelines for the students to follow (see Blackline #44 Project/Interview Day Procedures). If you have parent volunteers available, you may schedule them for this time to assist students. Another pair of hands is always helpful, especially if you do not want your interviews interrupted.

Maintaining work logs

Maintaining the work logs means faithfully checking them against our own must-do tracking binder where we have recorded all the completed tasks of required work during activity time. For each round of four weeks, we hand out a new work log sheet. We change the colour of the forms each month. They are kept in individual student duotangs for the year. At the end of the year they can be placed in the student's portfolio. Work logs are a useful tool for children to review what has been done each day, each week and each month, and when placed in the portfolio, with work samples, they become a testament to the work each child accomplishes throughout the year.

Long term projects

In the dynamic teaching model, students are encouraged to take on long term projects. They work on projects such as animal research, drama production, story writing or inventions research. Project work has many benefits. Students feel empowered to explore areas of interest. They practice the inquiry model of research, and they practice following through on a commitment. Though there will always be required curriculum topics which have to be covered in any given class, there is never a shortage of quality tasks which go beyond the basic requirements. Teachers are often concerned about what the adept students will do when they are finished their work. This is never a problem in this model because of the self-directed learning which takes place the whole year through. We provide students with specific projects such as a country to research, a picture book project, a novel study project, and a human body system project. Once they have completed these basic project requirements we provide them with the format to design their own project. (See the "plan your own project" sheet on the following page which helps students to formulate and organize their plan.) As students are eager to follow through with their learning and projects right to the end of the school year no one has to feel at loose ends when required work has been completed.

Organization

Be organized! The biggest factor in keeping a dynamic classroom running smoothly is organization. Maybe we should have called this book "The Organization Book" because a good part of it is about organization. So often when we have had visitors their most profound realization is how organized everything has to be. For all of you who asked, "Please, teach me how to be this organized?" we hope this book will help.

As mentioned in Chapter 8: Classroom Management and Organization, labelling everything in the room is important as a starting point. Preparing evaluation binders as soon as you have your class list gets you ready for the year and you can start observations as soon as those faces grace the classroom door. Putting a job list in place gets the students involved right away and

Plan Your Own Project

Choose to do a project on one of the following areas:

- ❏ Animals
- ❏ Plants
- ❏ The Environment
- ☑ Biomes

- ❏ Sports
- ❏ Novels, Stories, Books
- ❏ Science
- ❏ Other

What is the topic that you are going to research?

What has been happening to RAINFORESTS?

What resources are you going to use? *books* *CD on rainforest* *Internet* *encyclopedia* *filmstrip*	What are some of the questions you are going to answer? *What is a rainforest?* *Which animals live there?* *What kind of plants are there?* *Why are rainforests important?* *Who is damaging them?*
In what style are you going to publish your work? *poster*	
By: *Helga* Approved by: Date: *Jan. 3/05* *Mrs. B*	

leaves you to do other things. Once all of the organizational strategies are in place and working, you'll be finding ways to keep making the systems better.

Look ahead

After you have one cycle of centres under way, look ahead to the outcomes you'd like to achieve and choose your next centres. Make a list and keep it handy (see Blackline Master #8). This helps you decide which materials you will have to prepare and what lessons will need to be given in advance of those centres being opened. Block in the necessary lessons and prepare as much material as possible in advance. It is useful to have a file cabinet dedicated to files for each centre where you can store report forms, and task cards. Your storehouse of materials will grow month by month and you will have it for future years. Follow these guidelines and you will always be ahead of the game instead of trying to play catch up.

....

The beauty of this model, we jokingly say, is that "It runs itself". We can be interrupted by visitors, step out of the room, or become involved with a small group off to the side, and everything else keeps going. Substitute teachers marvel at the ease with which they can step into our shoes. When things are running smoothly, our roles shift from that of trainer and teacher to facilitator.

CHAPTER 14

CONCLUSION

In the province of the mind,
what one believes to be true
either is true or becomes true.
—— *JOHN LILY*

Optimism is the faith that leads to achievement.
Nothing can be done without hope and confidence.
——*HELEN KELLER*

Building a dynamic teaching model is an endeavour which takes a number of years and a true belief in this process. However, we can attest it is the most rewarding and exciting teaching we have ever experienced. We believe that the components of this model promote lifelong learning in students and ourselves.

The model we have described here in *Classroom of Choice* reflects the development of the strategies we employ as we continue to refine our understanding of how children learn best. We feel that adopting the dynamic teaching model in slow and steady stages is key to successful implementation. The experience and confidence gained at each stage will allow a teacher to move comfortably into the next stage. It took us several years to develop all the strategies we use and we recommend you take time to build your own.

By following the steps and guidelines we have provided in this book, teachers will be able to design their own dynamic teaching classroom with a minimum of bumps and scrapes. Everything provided in these pages has been classroom tested and refined to meet our standards. Not only have we assessed their usability but we have had our students give us feedback. So far these critics have been enthusiastic and positive.

There are a few things for which we could not make a blackline master or develop a strategy. Timing is a key factor in successful teaching. Knowing when to introduce new materials, when to review, when to move on and when to change something that doesn't work is a critical part of a teacher's daily decision-making. It is the teacher's talent, experience, instinct, and assessment skills which foster his/her ability to time things right. Teaching in a dynamic model requires more flexibility than in a traditional model, allowing teachers to capitalize on teachable moments when they arise. Waiting for just the right moment before introducing a new component of the curriculum requires patience and a sense of timing. We have experienced wonderful learning events when we have waited for students to ask for centre materials or a strategy to be put in place. It often was something we were holding back and needed to find just the right time to introduce though we are quite happy to let children think they got the idea first.

Though the schedule has a framework, there is plenty of room for it to be moulded and changed to meet the current needs of the children. This may also be the time when students are allowed to lead and make choices about what learning will take place next. Deviations from the schedule will not lead to chaos when children are involved in the decision-making of schedule changes and feel they have some control. As long as they are apprised of the changes to come, they seem quite able to handle the deviations from the norm. We have found that the use of a daily posted schedule usually provides children with enough information to suit their needs.

All the components we have described have an influence on the total classroom environment and events. Everything in a classroom is interconnected, as is true in any ecosystem. In the dynamic classroom, the environment, the students, the teachers, the parents, the administrators, and the curriculum are interdependent and interconnected. Educators need to be aware of this interconnectedness as they adopt and adapt the strategies described here.

Last but not least we have a lot of fun. Every day that we share with our students is a treat. We are able to use all of our creativity in the things we do. We witness tremendous growth and development in our students. Witnessing such changes in our students is the powerful experience which drives us to further refine our dynamic teaching model.

AFTERWORD

What better way to test the success of your teaching and feel like you are making a difference than to hear feedback right from the most important participants, the students. We ask children not only to reflect on their learning in math, science, writing, etc. but also to reflect on our classroom and what it means to them. We get them to tell us what makes it work for them and how it compares to their other learning experiences. They take this task very earnestly. We would like to leave you with a few of their thoughts.

I enjoy this class because we all get to help each other whether we're in grade four, three, or two. I think we can learn from each other and working in a group of different ages is a great experience. It was fun watching each group perform their dance.
— Fatima, age 10

Last year in grade 2, me and my best friend, Sara did country research on Costa Rica. It was really fun! I liked working with my friend, Kim when it was partner time, like in science or technology experiments.
— Maria, age 8

I remember when I could not finish my centres, and now I got a Fantastic News!. And now I am done all my centres.
— Pawel, age 9

This year I liked the math block centre because we had to fill out puzzles with tangrams like the "running man" puzzle.
— Mikos, age 10

What I accomplished this year was a four part story.
— Helga, age 9

I remember finishing my first story.
— Brian, age 7

I really like doing my story because I like creating things and using my ideas for them.
— Jenn, age 9

I will always remember doing novel study with the book, "Anne of Green Gables" because it was such a large book and it took so long to finish it and same with the project.
But I finished it just in time!
— Lisa, age 8

I remember doing my first book, "The Girl With Square Eyes". I had a lot of fun and I felt I did so well on it that I gave it one of my portfolio prides. In my opinion, it was one of the best stories I ever wrote. Soon after I wrote another story. I wrote it with a partner. We wrote a joke book called, "Just for Laughs"
—Sook-i, age 10

My best project was country research because I did lots of work on it.
— Greta, age 8

I liked helping Scott with his work when he was stuck.
— Oran, age 7

My favourite job was "our news" because I always wrote a lot and I like to hear what other people did. This year I was finally in grade four. I just wish I did not have to leave this class next year.
— Claire, age 10

I was really excited when I published my first story.
My favourite thing that I did this year was doing my weather project and doing my desert project. The new thing that I did this year was getting to be chairperson.
— Sanna, age 7

I liked it when we did our project on Canada. I liked it when we brainstormed our ideas.
— Kathy, age 10

Sometimes I like doing things with grade twos because you can help them like you are old.
— Marg, age 10

When I had five centres to do on catch-up day, I finished.
— Paul, age 9

REFERENCES AND RECOMMENDED READING

To help you locate reading resources that suit your needs, we have organized our recommended reading list into four categories:

Evaluation and Assessment
Multiage Teaching
Reading, Writing, and Literacy
Theory, Philosophy and Other Stuff

These resources are recommended because we believe that they will expand any teacher's knowledge of pedagogical theory and practice and facilitate the change towards the dynamic teaching model.

Evaluation and Assessment

Au, K.H., Scheu, J.A., Kawakami, A.J., & Herman, P.A. (1990). Assessment and accountability in a whole literacy curriculum. *The Reading Teacher, 43*(8), 574-578.

Anthony, R., Johnson, T., Mickelson, N., & Preece, A. (1991). *Evaluating Literacy: A Perspective for Change.* Portsmouth, NH: Heinemann Publishers.

Barrs. M. (1990). The Primary Language Record: Reflection of Issues in Evaluation. *Language Arts, 67*(3), 244-253.

Baskwill, J., & Whitman, P. (1988). *Evaluation: Whole Language, Whole Child.* New York: Scholastic.

Cambourne, B., & Turnbill, J. (1990). Assessment in whole language classrooms: Theory into practice. *The Elementary School Journal, 90*(3).

Chittendon, E.A., & Courtney, R. (1989). Assessment of young children's reading: Documentation as an alternative to testing. In D.S. Strickland, & L.M. Morrow (Eds.), *Emerging Literacy: Young Children Learn to Read and Write.* Newark, DE: International Reading Association.

Clay, M. M. (1985). *The Early Detection of Reading Difficulties.* Aukland and Portsmouth, NH: Heinemann Publishers.

Clay, M. M. (1993). *An Observation Survey of Early LIteracy Achievement.* Portsmouth, NH: Heinemann Publishers.

Clemmons, J., Laase, L., Cooper, D., Areglado, N. & Dill, M. (1993). *Portfolios in the Classroom: A Teacher's Sourcebook.* New York: Scholastic.

Cochrane, O. & Cochrane, D. (1992). *Whole Language Evaluation for Classrooms.* Winnipeg, MB: Whole Language Consultants.

Drummond, M. J. (1994). *Learning to See: Assessment through Observation.* Markham, ON: Pembroke Publishers.

Flood, J., & Lapp, D. (1989). Reporting reading progress: A comparison portfolio for parents. *The Reading Teacher, 42*(7), 508-514.

Gentry, J. R., (1987). *Spel...Is a Four-Letter Word.* Richmond Hill, ON: Scholastic Canada.

Goodman, K. (1986). *What's Whole in Whole Language?* Portsmouth, NH: Heinemann Publishers.

Goodman, K. (1989). *The Whole Language Evaluation Book.* Portsmouth, NH: Heinemann Publishers.

Goodman, Y. (1985). Kidwatching: Observing children in the classroom. In A. Jaggar, & M.T. Smith-Burke (Eds.), *Observing the Language Learner,* Newark, DE: International Reading Association/National Council of Teachers of English.

Goodman, Y., Watson, D., & Burke, C. (1987). *Reading Miscue Inventory: Alternative Procedures,* New York: Richard C. Owen Publishers.

Graves, D. H. & Sunstein, S. (Eds.) *Portfolio Portraits.* Portsmouth, NH: Heinemann Publishers.

Gronlund, N. E. (1981). *Measurement and Evaluation in Teaching.* (4th ed.) New York: Macmillan.

Halsall, N. & Wall, C. (1992). Pedagogical Practices in French Immersion and Regular English Programs. *The Canadian Modern Language Review, 49*(1), 60-79.

Halsall, N. & Wall, C. (1994). Assessing child centeredness in French immersion classrooms. *The Canadian School Executive, 13*(9), 19-21.

Harp, B. (Ed.) (1991). *Assessment and Evaluation in Whole Language Programs, Revised Edition.* Norwood, MA: Christopher-Gordon Publishers.

Johnston, P. (1986). The process of assessment in language arts. In J.R. Squires (Ed.), *The Dynamics of Language Learning: Research in Reading and English.*

Johnston, P. (1987). Teachers as evaluation experts. *The Reading Teacher, 40*(8), 744-748.

Mathews, J.K. (1990). From computer management to portfolio assessment. *The Reading Teacher, 43*(6), 420-421.

Norris. D. & Bouchard, J. (1980). *Observing Children.* Toronto: Toronto Board of Education.

North York Board of Education, Curriculum and Staff Development Services. (1983). *LOOK! HEAR! Developing Programs for Primary Children Based on Observations of Learning Needs.* North York: North York Board of Education.

Picciotto, L. P. (1992). *Evaluation: A Team Effort.* Richmond Hill, ON: Scholastic Canada.

Picciotto, L. P. (1996). *Student-Led Parent Conferences: How to Launch and Manage Conferences that Get Parents Involved and Improve Student Learning.* Richmond Hill, ON: Scholastic Canada.

Sullivan, M. (1995). *Making Portfolio Assessment Easy: Reproducible Forms and Checklists and Strategies for Using Them.* Richmond Hill, ON: Scholastic Canada.

Wason-Ellam, L. (1994). *Literacy Moments to Report Cards*. Markham, ON: Pembroke Publishers.

Winograd, P., Paris, S., & Bridge, C. (1991). Improving the assessment of literacy. *The Reading Teacher, 45*(2), 108-116.

Multi-age Teaching

Anderson, R. H. & Pavan, B. N. (1993). *Nongradedness: Helping It to Happen*. Lancaster, PA: Technomic Publishing Company.

Bingham, A. A. et al. (1995). *Exploring the Multiage Classroom*. York, MA: Stenhouse Publishers.

Cushman, K. (1990). The whys and hows of the multi-age primary classroom. *American Educator, 14*(2) 28-32 and 39.

Gajadharsingh, J. (1991). *The Multi-Grade Classroom: Myth and Reality, A Canadian Study*. Toronto: Canadian Education Association.

Gaustad, J. (1994). *Non-Graded Education: Overcoming Obstacles to Implementing the Multiage Classroom*. Oregon School Study Council, 38 (3) & (4).

Giles, J. (1997). Multi-age Family Groupings - Questions and Answers. *OPSTF News, 11*(5), 10-13.

Goodlad, J. I. & Anderson, R. H. (1987). *The Non-Graded Elementary School. rev. ed.* New York: Teachers College Press.

Grant, J. & Johnson, B. (1994). *A Common Sense Guide to Multiage Practices*. Columbus, OH: Teachers' Publishing Group.

Halliwell, J. W. (1963). A comparison of pupil achievement in graded and non-graded primary classrooms. *Journal of Experimental Education.* 32(1), 59-66.

Hammack, B. G. (1974). *Self-concept: Evaluation of preschool children in single and multi-age classroom settings.* Unpublished doctoral dissertation, Texas Women's University. *Dissertation Abstracts International, 35*(10), 6572-6573.

Kasten, W. C. & Clarke, B. (1993). *The Multi-Age Classroom: A Family of Learners*. Katonah, New York: Richard C. Owen Publishers.

Katz, L., Evangelou, D. & Hartman, J. A. (1990). *The Case for Mixed-Age Grouping in Early Education*. Washington, DC: National Association for the Education of Young Children.

McClay, J. L. (1996). *The Multiage Classroom*. Westminster, CA: Teacher Created Materials.

Milburn, D. (1981). A study of multi-age or family grouped classrooms. *Phi Delta Kappan, 62*(7), 513-514.

n.a.m.e. National Alliance of Multiage Educators, *A Newsletter for Educators*. Peterborough, NH: The Society for Developmental Education.

Rathbone, C., Bingham, A., Dorta, P., McClaskey, M. & O'Keefe, J. (1993). *Multiage Portraits, Teaching and Learning in Mixed-age Classrooms*. Peterborough, NH: Crystal Springs Books.

Schrankler, W. J. (1976). Family grouping and the affective domain. *Elementary School Journal, 76*(7), 432-439.

The Society for Developmental Education. (1993). *Multiage Classrooms: The Ungrading of America's Schools, The Multiage Resource Book*. Peterborough, NH: Crystal Springs Books.

The Society for Developmental Education. (1996). *Multiage Handbook: A Comprehensive Resource for Multiage Practices*. Peterborough, NH: Crystal Springs Books.

Reading, Writing, and Literacy

Altwerger, B., Edelsky, C., & Flores, B.M. (1987). Whole language: What's new? *The Reading Teacher, 41*(2), 144-154.

Atwell, N. (1989). *Coming to Know: Writing to Learn in the Intermediate Grades*. Portsmouth, NH: Heinemann Publishers.

Atwell, N. (1991). *Side by Side: Essays on Teaching to Learn*. Portsmouth, NH: Heinemann Publishers.

Barrett, F. L. (1988). *A Teacher's Guide to Shared Reading*. Richmond Hill, ON: Scholastic Canada.

Barton, B. & Booth, D. (1990). *Stories in the Classroom*. Markham, ON: Pembroke Publishers.

Baskwill, J. & Whitman, P. (1986). *Whole Language Sourcebook*. Richmond Hill, ON: Scholastic Canada.

Baskwill, J. & Whitman, P. (1988). *A Guide to Classroom Publishing*. Richmond Hill, ON: Scholastic Canada.

Booth, D. & Lundy, C. (1985). *Improvisations: Learning Through Drama*. Toronto, ON: Harcourt Brace and Company.

Booth, D. (1994). *Classroom Voices: Language-Based Learning in the Elementary School*. Toronto: Harcourt Brace Canada.

Brown, H. & Cambourne, B. (1989). *Read and Retell: A Strategy for the Whole Language/Natural Learning Classroom*. Portsmouth, NH: Heinemann Publishers.

Butler, A. & Turnbill, J. (1986). *Towards a Reading-Writing Classroom*. Orwell, New South Wales, Australia: Primary English Teaching Association/Irwin Publishing.

Calkins, L. M. (1983). *Lessons from a Child*. Portsmouth, NH: Heinemann Publishers.

Calkins, L. M. (1994). *The Art of Teachng Writing, New Edition*. Portsmouth, NH: Heinemann Publishers.

Calkins, L. M. & Harwayne, S. (1991). *Living Between the Lines*. Toronto, ON: Irwin Publishing.

Cambourne, B. (1988). *The Whole Story: Natural Learning and the Acquisition of Literacy in the Classroom*. Richmond Hill, ON: Scholastic Canada.

Clay, M. M. (1991). *Becoming Literate: The Construction of Inner Control.* Portsmouth, NH: Heinemann Publishers.

Cochrane, O. et al. (1984). *Reading, Writing and Caring.* Winnipeg, MB: Whole Language Consultants Ltd.

Crafton, L. K. (1991). *Whole Language... Moving Forward.* Katonah, NY: Richard C. Owen Publishers.

Forester, A. D. & Reinhard, M. (1989). *The Learner's Way.* Winnipeg, MB: Peguis Publishers.

Forester, A. D. & Reinhard, M. (1991). *On the Move: Teaching the Learner's Way in Grades 4-6.* Winnipeg, MB: Peguis Publishers.

Gentry, R. (1987). *Spel...is a Four-Letter Word.* Portsmouth, NH: Heinemann Publishers.

Gentry, R. & Wallace-Gillet, J. (1992). *Teaching Kids to Spell.* Portsmouth, NH: Heinemann Publishers.

Graves, D. H. (1983). *Writing: Teachers and Children at Work.* Portsmouth, NH: Heinemann Publishers.

Graves, D. H. (1989). *Discover Your Own Literacy.* Toronto, ON: Irwin Publishing.

Graves, D. H. (1991). *Build a Literate Classroom.* Toronto, ON: Irwin Publishing.

Hall, N. (1987). *The Emergence of Literacy.* Exeter, NH: Heinemann Publishers.

Hansen, J. (1987). *When Writers Read.* Toronto, ON: Irwin Publishing.

Harste, J., Short, K., & Burke, C. (1988). *Creating Classrooms for Authors: The Reading-Writing Connection.* Portsmouth, NH: Heineman Publishers.

Harste, J., Woodward, V., & Burke, C. *Language Stories and Literacy Lessons.* Exeter, NH: Heinemann Publishers.

Hart-Hewins, L. & Wells, J. (1990). *Real Books for Reading.* Markham, ON: Pembroke Publishers.

Harwayne, S. (1992). *Lasting Impressions: Weaving Literature into the Writing Workshop.* Portsmouth, NH: Heinemann Publishers.

Heald-Taylor, G. (1989). *The Administrator's Guide to Whole Language.* Ketonah, NY: Richard C. Owen Publishers.

Holdaway, D. (1979). *The Foundations of Literacy.* Richmond Hill, ON: Scholastic-TAB Publications.

Jackson, N. R. (1992). *The Reading-Writing Workshop: Getting Started.* Richmond Hill, ON: Scholastic Canada.

Johnson, T. D. & Louis, D. R. (1987). *Literacy through Literature.* Richmond Hill, ON: Scholastic-TAB Publications.

Johnson, T. D. & Louis, D. R. (1990). *Bringing It All Together: A Program for Literacy.* Richmond Hill, ON: Scholastic-TAB Publications.

Massam, J. & Kulk, A. (1986). *And What Else?* New Zealand: Shortland Publishing.

Newman, J. (1984). *The Craft of Children's Writing*. Richmond Hill, ON: Scholastic-TAB Publications.

Newman, J. (1985). *Whole Language: Theory in Use*. Portsmouth, NH: Heinemann Publishers.

North York Board of Education, Curriculum and Staff Development Services. (1987). *Active Learning, Teaching and Learning in the Junior Division*. North York: North York Board of Education.

Ontario Ministry of Education and and Ontario Public School Teachers' Federation. (1986). *Ages 9 Through 12: A Resource Book for Teachers, a Support Document to the Formative Years*. Toronto: Ontario Ministry of Education and Ontario Public School Teachers' Federation.

Peterson, R. & Eedds, M. (1990). *Grand Conversations: Literature Groups in Action*. Richmond Hill, ON: Scholastic Canada.

Phenix, J. (1990). *Teaching Writing*. Markham, ON: Pembroke Publishers.

Phenix, J. & Scott-Dunne, D. (1994). *Spelling for Parents*. Markham, ON: Pembroke Publishers.

Phenix, J. & Scott-Dunne, D. (1991). *Spelling Instruction that Makes Sense*. Markham, ON: Pembroke Publishers.

Routman, R. (1988). *Transitions: From Literature to Literacy*. Portsmouth, NH: Heinemann Pubishers.

Routman, R. (1991). *Invitations: Changing as Teachers and Learners K-12*. Toronto, ON: Irwin Publishing.

Schwartz, S. (1987). *All Write! A Teacher's Guide to Writing, Grades K-6*. Toronto, ON: OISE Press.

Schwartz, S. & Pollishuke, M. (1990). *Creating the Child-Centred Classroom*. Toronto, ON: Irwin Publishing.

Schwartz. S. & Bone, M. (1995). *Retelling, Relating, Reflecting: Beyond the Three R's*. Toronto, ON: Irwin Publishing.

Short, K. O. & Mitchell Pierce, K. (1990). *Talking About Books: Creating Literate Communities*. Toronto, ON: Irwin Publishing.

Smith, F. (1982). *Writing and the Writer.* New York: Holt, Rinehart and Winston.

Smith, F. (1985). *Reading Without Nonsense*. New York: Teachers College Press.

Smith, F. (1986). *Insult to Intelligence*. Portsmouth, New Hampshire: Heinemann Publishers.

Strickland, D. & Morrow, L. M. (Eds.) (1989). *Emerging Literacy: Young Children Learn to Read and Write*. Newark, DE: International Reading Association.

Trelease, Jim. (1985). *The Read-Aloud Handbook, Revised Edition*. New York, NY: Viking/Penguin.

Watson, D. (1987). *Ideas and Insights: Language Arts in the Elementary School.* Urbana, IL: National Council of Teachers of English.

Weaver, C. (1994). *Reading Process and Practice: From Socio-Psycholinguistics to Whole Language, Second Edition.* Portsmouth, NH: Heinemann Publishers.

Wells, G. (1986). *The Meaning Makers: Children Learning Language and Using Language to Learn.* Portsmouth, NH: Heinemann Publishers.

Wilde, S. (1991). *You Kan Red This!: Spelling and Punctuation for Whole Language Classrooms, K-6.* Portsmouth, NH: Heinemann Publishers.

Zarry, L. (1992). *Literacy Through Whole Language.* Winnipeg, MB: Peguis Publishers.

Theory, Philosophy and Other Stuff

Airasian, P.W. & Walsh, M.E. (1997). Constructivist Cautions, *Phi Delta Kappan.* February, 444-449.

Bruner, J. (1977). *The Process of Education.* Cambridge, MA: Harvard University Press

Combs, A.W. (1982). *A personal approach to teaching: Beliefs that make a difference.* Boston, MA: Allyn and Bacon, Inc.

Fullan, M. (1993). *Change Forces: Probing the Depths of Educational Reform.* London, GB: The Falmer Press.

Gardner, H. (1983). *Frames of Mind: The Theory of Multiple Intelligences.* New York: Basic Books.

Gardner, H. (1993). *Multiple Intelligences: The Theory in Practice.* New York: Basic Books.

Ginsburg, H. & Opper, S. (1979). *Piaget's Theory of Intellectual Development.* (2nd ed.) Englewood Cliffs, NJ: Prentice-Hall, Inc.

Glasser, W. (1969). *Schools without Failure.* New York: Harper & Row.

Glasser, W. (1986). *Control Theory in the Classroom.* New York: Harper Collins Publishers.

Glasser, W. (1990). *The Quality School.* New York: Harper Collins Publishers.

Glasser, W. (1992). *The Quality School Teacher.* New York: Harper Collins Publishers.

Glasser, W. (1998). *Choice Theory, A New Psychology of Personal Freedom.* New York: Harper Collins Publishers.

Hart, L. A. (1992). *Human Brain and Human Learning.* Village of Oak Creek, AR: Books for Educators.

Knowles, M. (1975). *Self-directed learning: A guide for learners and teachers.* New York: Association Press.

Moll, L. C. (Ed.). (1990). *Vygotsky and Education: Instructional Implications and Applications of Sociohistorical Psychology.* Cambridge University Press.

National Association for the Education of Young Children. (1989). *Appropriate Education in the Primary Grades.* Washington, D.C.

Ontario Ministry of Education and Training. (1995). *The Common Curriculum: Policies and Outcomes, Grades 1-9.* Toronto, ON.

Piaget, J. (1952). *The Origins of Intelligence in Children* (M. Cook, Trans.). New York: International Universities Press.

Sternberg, R.J. (1990). Thinking styles: Keys to understanding student performance. *Phi Delta Kappan*, January, 367.

Vygotsky, L.S. (1962). *Thought and language.* Cambridge, MA: M.I.T. Press.

Vygotsky, L.S. (1978). Play and its role in mental development. *Soviet Psychology*, 12 (62).

Weininger, O. (1979). *Play and Education: The Basic Tool for Early Childhood Learning.* Springfield, Ill: Charles E. Thomas Publishers.

BLACKLINE MASTERS

These blackline masters may be photocopied by original purchaser of this book only.

Blackline masters may be used as models or as reference for creating your own.

Blacklines for Teacher Use

Blacklines for Student Use

Big Books Centre 	**Correspondence Centre** 	**Grammar Examiner Centre** 
Magnetic Board Centre 	**Poetry Study Centre** 	**Story Study Centre** 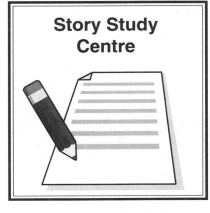
Book/Resource Centre 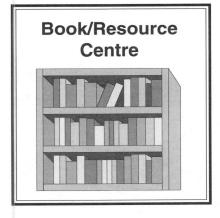	**Cursive Writing Centre** 	**Journal Writing Centre** 
Make-A-Book Centre 	**Shared Reading Centre** 	**Story Writing Centre** 

Chalkboard Centre

Flannel Board Centre

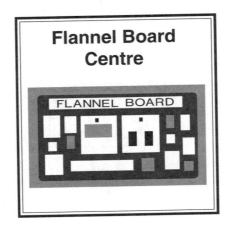

Novel Study Centre

Spelling Centre

Banking/Money Centre

Calendar Centre

Math Games Centre

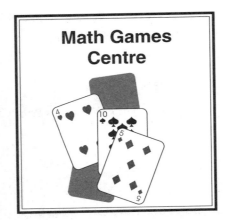

Puzzles Centre

Board Games Centre

Consumer Affairs Centre

Math Problems Centre

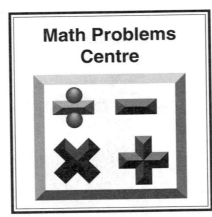

Math Centre

CLASSROOM OF CHOICE

Calculator Centre	Math Blocks Centre	Measurement Centre
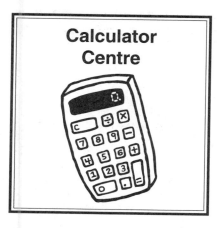		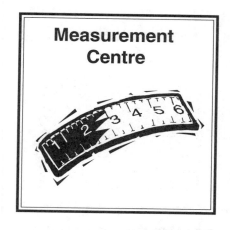
Sand Table Centre	Animal Research Centre	Water Table Centre
	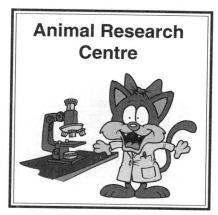	
Ecology Centre	Research Projects Centre	Weather Centre
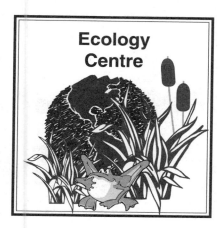	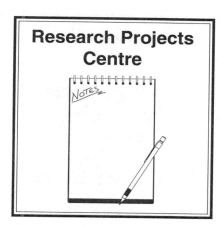	
Experiment Centre Centre	Science Centre	Inventions Centre
	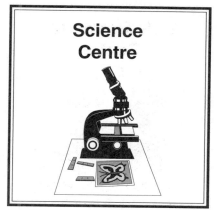	

Design-A-Solution Centre 	**Overhead Projector Centre** 	**Publishing Centre** 
Technology Tools Centre 	**Computer Centre** 	**Film Projector Centre** 
Poster Projects Centre 	**Tape Recording Centre** 	**Video Centre** 
Construction Centre 	**Newspaper Centre** 	**Audio Centre** 

Technology Centre	Media Centre	Art Centre

Drawing Centre	**Sculpture Centre**	**Dance Centre**

Music Centre	**Toys Centre**	**Drama Centre**

Painting Centre	**Canadiana Centre**	**Personal Well Being Centre**
		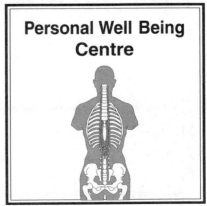

Cooking Centre	Map and Globe Centre	History Centre
	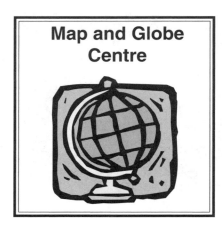	

Free Choice	Catch-up	School Library Pass

The Check-in System

The Centre Tickets

The Check-in System

The Name Cards

LIST OF CHOICES

- animal research
- art
- audio
- banking/money
- big books
- board games
- book/resource
- calculator
- calendar
- Canadiana
- chalkboard
- computers
- construction
- consumer affairs
- cooking
- correspondence
- cursive writing
- dance
- design a solution
- drama
- drawing
- ecology
- experiments
- film projector
- flannel board
- grammar examiner
- history
- inventions
- journal writing
- make-a-book
- magnetic board
- map and globe
- math
- math blocks
- math games
- math problems
- measurement
- media
- music
- newspaper
- novel study
- overhead projector
- paint easel
- personal well-being
- poetry study
- poster projects
- publishing centre
- puzzles
- research projects
- sand table
- science
- sculpture
- shared reading
- spelling
- story study
- story writing
- tape recording
- technology
- technology tools
- toys
- video
- water table
- weather

Centres for the Year

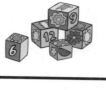 

Centres for the Year
•
•
•
•
•
•
•
•
•
•
•
•
•
•
•
•
•

Must-do Planning List

Period beginning: _____   Period ending: _____

Centre: Activity: Expectations:

_____

_____

_____

_____

_____

_____

_____

_____

_____

_____

_____

_____

_____

_____

_____

_____

_____

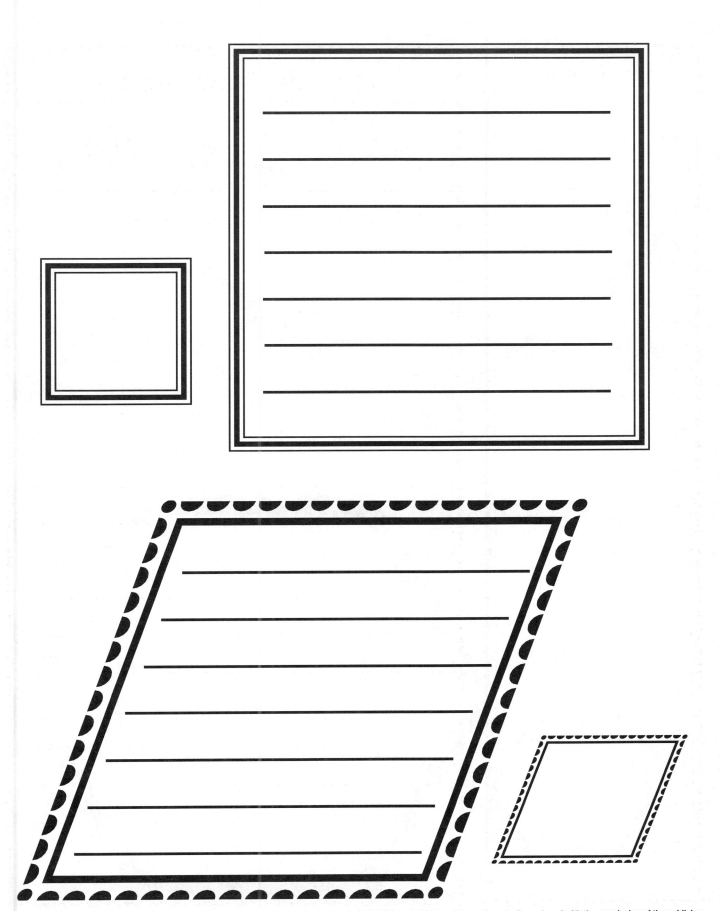

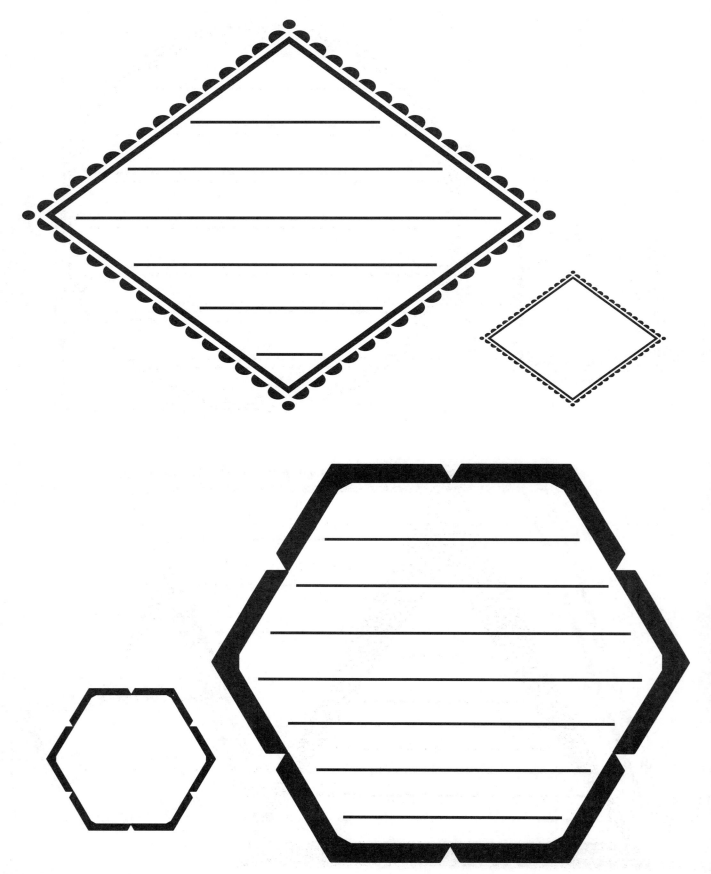

CLASSROOM OF CHOICE

	Circles
	Triangles
	Diamonds
	Hexagons
	Squares
	Parallelograms

CLASSROOM OF CHOICE

Daily Classroom Plans

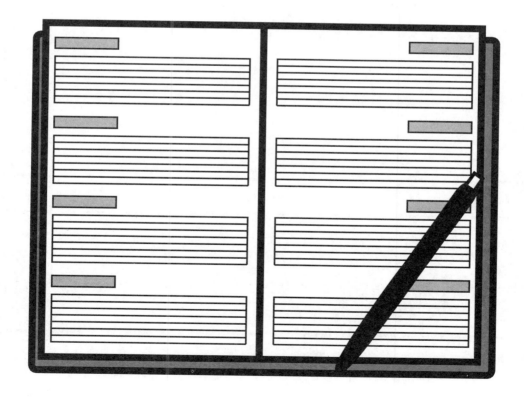

Date:

| |
| |

recess

| |
| |

lunch

| |
| |

recess

| |
| |

Reminders:

Time	Monday	Tuesday	Wednesday	Thursday	Friday
recess					
lunch					
recess					
clean-up and home time					

BLACKLINE MASTERS

Student Personal Records

Personal Records

Communication History

Student Name _____

Birthdate _____

Address _____

_____

Home Phone _____

Mother's Phone _____

Father's Phone _____

BLACKLINE MASTERS

Student Evaluation Records

Math, Spelling, Reading, Writing, Research

Observations

Name _____

MATH INTERVIEWS

Name: _____

Date: _____ **Strand:** _____

Target Concept: _____

What to look for:

-

-

-

-

-

-

-

-

-

-

-

-

Date: _____ **Strand:** _____

Target Concept: _____

Date: _____ **Strand:** _____

Target Concept: _____

MATH INTERVIEWS CONTINUED

Date: _____ Strand: _____

Target Concept: _____

Date: _____ Strand: _____

Target Concept: _____

Date: _____ Strand: _____

Target Concept: _____

READING INTERVIEWS

Name: _____

Date: _____

Title: _____

Level: _____

What to look for:

-
-
-
-
-
-
-
-
-
-
-
-

Date: _____

Title: _____

Level: _____

Date: _____

Title: _____

Level: _____

Date: _____

Title: _____

Level: _____

**READING INTERVIEWS
CONTINUED**

Date: _____ Level: _____

Title: _____

Date: _____ Level: _____

Title: _____ _____

WRITING INTERVIEWS

Name: _____

Date: _____ **Type:** _____

Title: _____

Date finished: _____

What to look for:

-
-
-
-
-
-
-
-
-
-
-
-

Date: _____ **Type:** _____

Title: _____

Date finished: _____

Date: _____ **Type:** _____

Title: _____

Date finished: _____

Date: _____ Type: _____

Title: _____

Date finished: _____

WRITING INTERVIEWS CONTINUED

Date: _____ Type: _____

Title: _____

Date finished: _____

Date: _____ Type: _____

Title: _____

Date finished: _____

ANIMAL RESEARCH

Project Update	Animal	Start Date	Date	Progress	Finish Date	Product

RESEARCH

Project Update	Topic	Start Date	Date	Progress	Finish Date	Product

BLACKLINE MASTERS

STORY WRITING Project Update	Title	Start Date	Date	Progress	Finish Date	Product

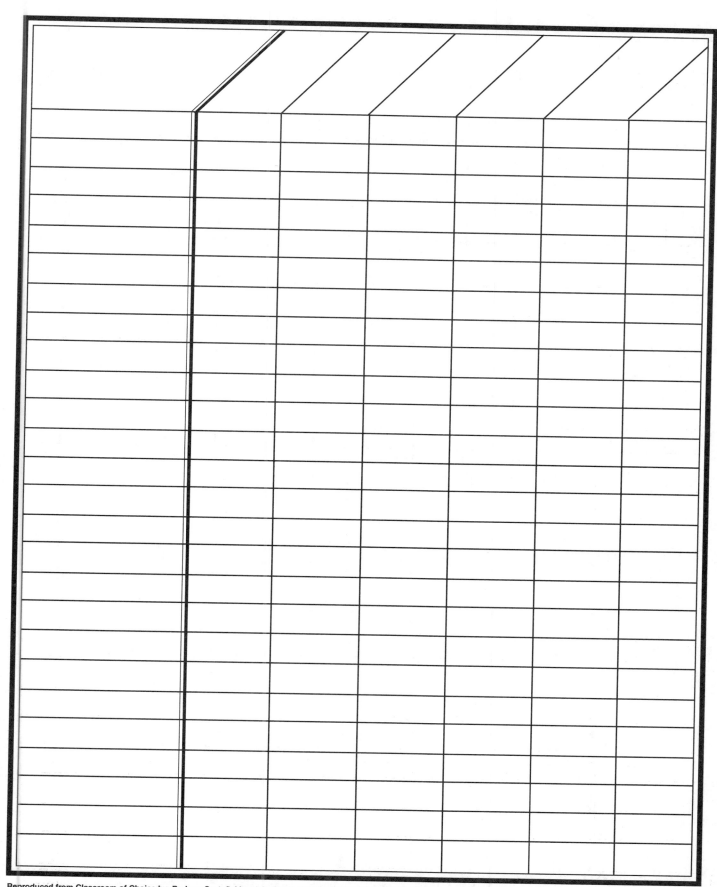

BLACKLINE MASTERS

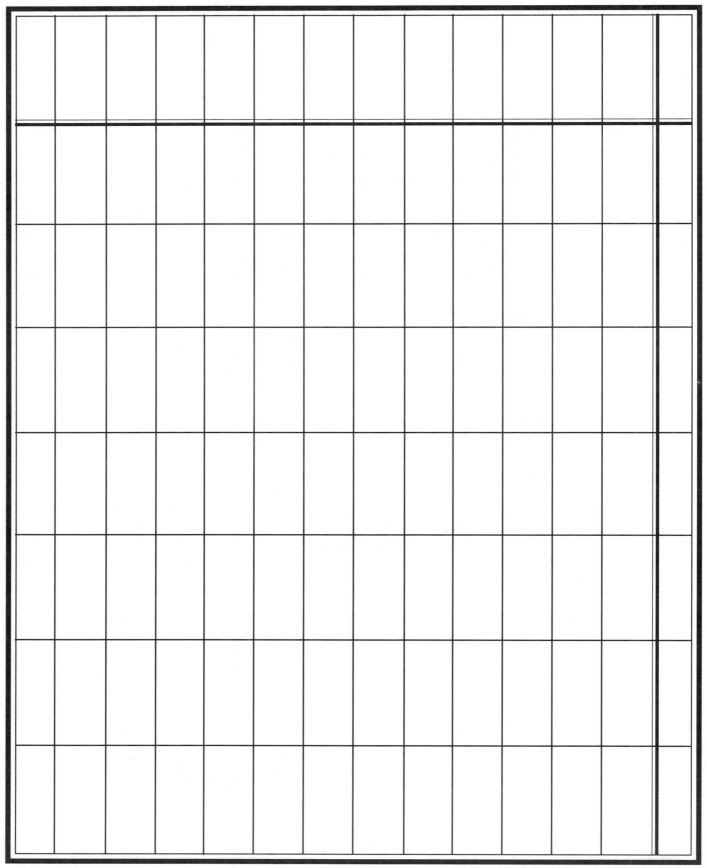

CLASSROOM OF CHOICE

Must-do Centre Marking

BLACKLINE MASTERS

ART CENTRES

LANGUAGE CENTRES

BLACKLINE MASTERS

MATH CENTRES

SCIENCE CENTRES

BLACKLINE MASTERS

SELF AND SOCIETY CENTRES						

CLASSROOM OF CHOICE

TECHNOLOGY/ MULTIMEDIA CENTRES						

BLACKLINE MASTERS

Classroom Overheads

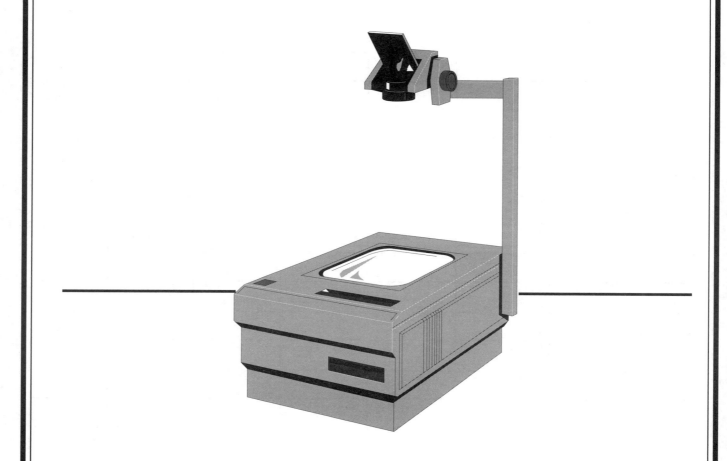

TARGET _____

				CRITERIA
				1
				2
				3
				4

Fabulous News!

You have been signed off your work log for four different weeks. That means you have worked hard on your centres, you are organized, and always on the job! Congratulations!

_____

Date _____   **From,** _____

Fantastic News!

_____

You have finished all of your centres for this round. That means you have worked hard on your centres, you are organized, and always on the job! Until more people are finished you will have FREE CHOICE. Congratulations!

Date _____   **From,** _____

Great News!

You have finished all of your centres for one week and have gotten your work log signed off. Keep up the good work!

Date _____   From, _____

Good News!

You have finished all of your centres for one week and have gotten your work log signed off. Keep up the good work!

Date _____   From, _____

Champion Classroom Cleaners!

Will help clean up:

1. every group table and push in chairs
2. every centre bucket and activity cards
3. every book bucket
4. art supplies and art table
5. all lunch messes
6. the book/resource corner
7. the FLOOR!
8. all the other activity centres around the room
9. the coat area in the hallway
10. their tickets after activity centres and return them

The Duties of the Group Leader

1. Help people remember to sign their work logs.
2. Get the centre materials and organize your group for the activity.
3. Organize your group for tidy-up time and check your table.
4. Hand-out notebooks or papers.
5. Be helpful to your group.
6. Do extra jobs for the teachers.

Project Interview Day

Procedures:

1. Check your work log and unfinished work list.
2. Finish all must-do work and hand it in.
3. Work on any unfinished writing or projects (see list of priorities).
4. Do not disturb the teachers! They will be interviewing students on reading, writing and math. This is very important.
5. If you need something or need help, get someone in your group or class to help, or go on to something else.

How To Do Quality Work

1. Record the date.
2. Record the title.
3. Include the centre, activity and level.
4. Write in full sentences.
5. Write on lines and neatly.
6. Use the card for correct spelling.
7. Read your resources.
8. Write the information in your own words.
9. Use all available space on the pages.
10. Include diagrams that are labelled and coloured.
11. Check for corrections and additions.
12. Glue folded papers into books.
13. Add the date and centre name on the outside of the folded paper.

Rainy Day Activities

Choose from:

1. audio centre
2. big books
3. book corner
4. construction blocks
5. math blocks
6. drawing centre
7. puzzles
8. board games
9. unfinished work

Procedures

for doing must-do centres:

1. Check your group assignment.
2. Pick up your work log.
3. Place your tickets in the proper pockets.
4. Get the centre tub to your table.
5. READ! the activity cards.
6. CHOOSE! the activity level you need.
7. SIGN! your work log.
8. Record the title, date and centre name on all of your work.
9. Number questions and record in full sentences.
10. Glue sheets in appropriate books, finished or not finished.
11. Hand in finished work.
    Take unfinished work for homework.
12. Tidy up and sign off.

You should tell on someone when:

1. they are seriously injuring someone.
2. they might hurt themselves.
3. they are damaging property.

If you have a problem with  someone ...

do the following:

1. Ask the person to "Please, stop," and tell him/her why.

2. Move away.

3. Go and tell one of the teachers.

No Clowning Carpet Credo

1. Sit cross-legged.
2. Hands in your lap.
3. Zip up your mouth.
4. Look at the speaker.
5. Listen.

Proper Lunchtime Behaviour

1. Stay seated with your feet on the floor.
2. Talk to your group quietly.
3. Don't talk with your mouth full.
4. Leave your place clean.
5. Go when you are dismissed.

BLACKLINE MASTERS

Good Day!

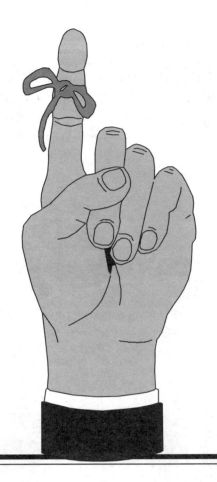

Remember . . .

- a pencil
- an eraser
- your shoes
- your homework
- change your ticket
- think, think, think!

Our Writers' Wall

The Art Gallery

LOOK!

but

DON'T

TOUCH,

please.

BLACKLINE MASTERS

Fold here for placement on table.

Sssh!
Do not disturb,
please.

Interview
being held.

Fold here for placement on table.

Please do not disturb!

Conference
in progress

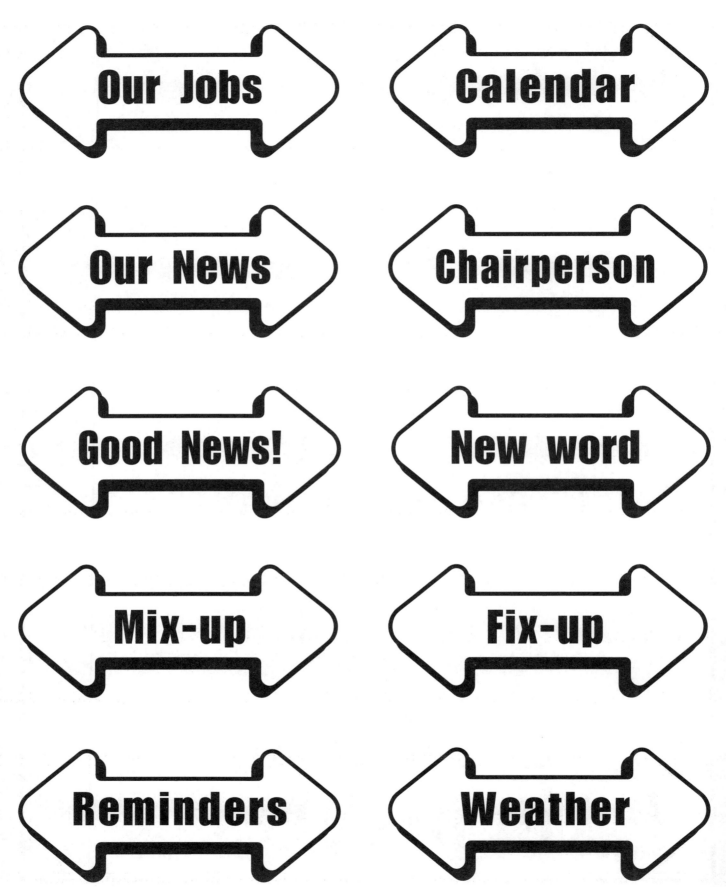

Our Jobs

Calendar

Our News

Chairperson

Good News!

New word

Mix-up

Fix-up

Reminders

Weather

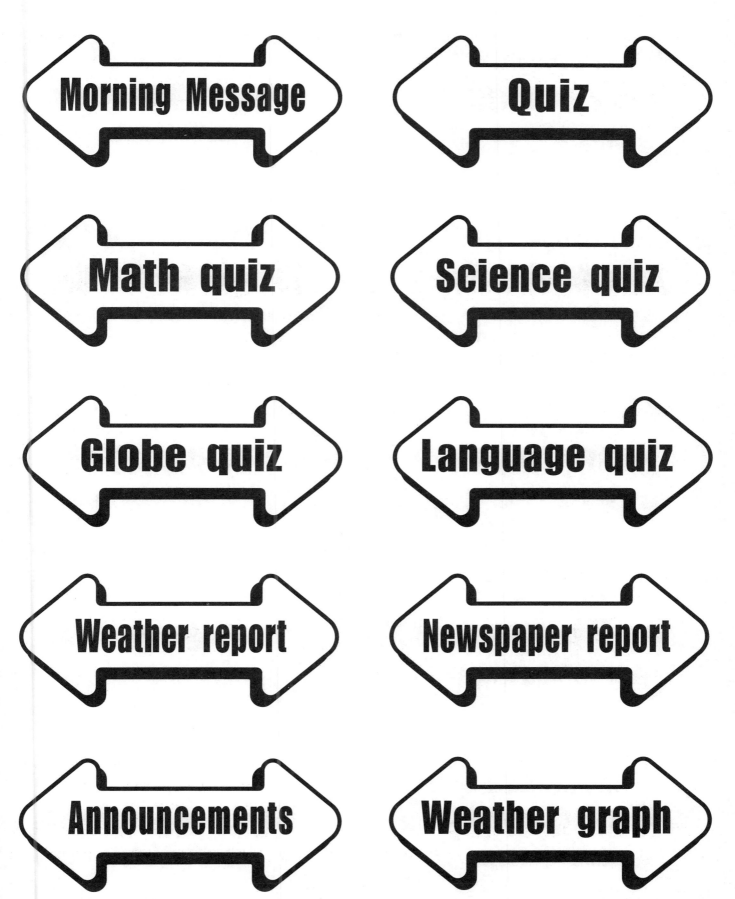

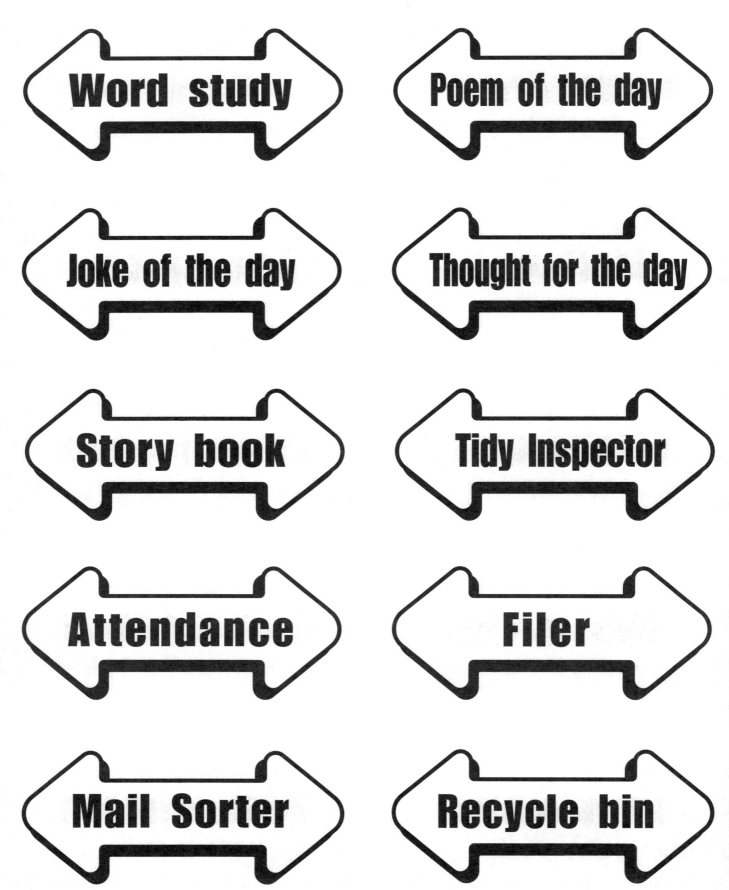

Word study

Poem of the day

Joke of the day

Thought for the day

Story book

Tidy Inspector

Attendance

Filer

Mail Sorter

Recycle bin

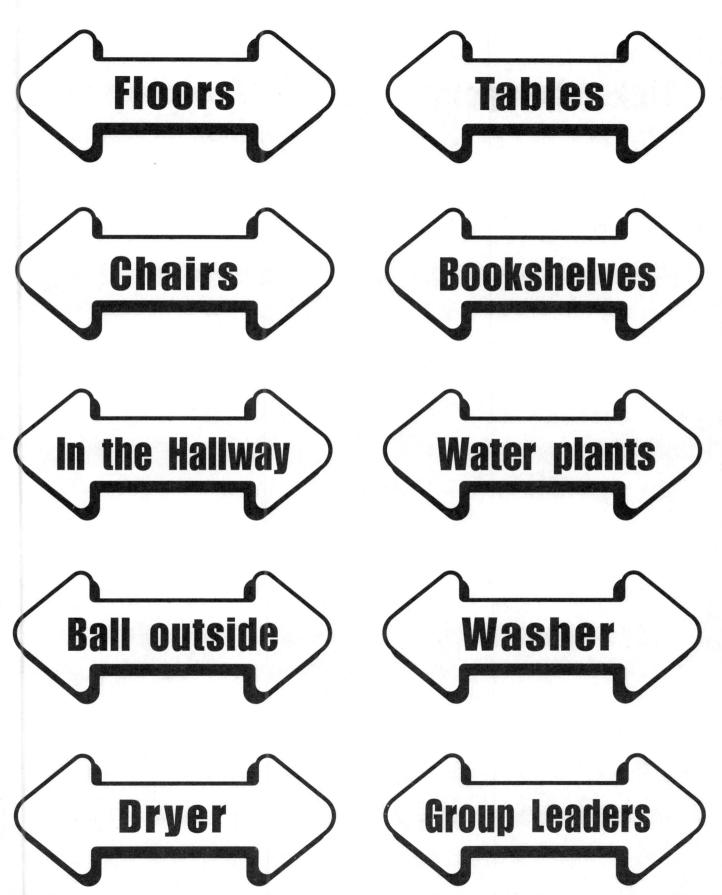

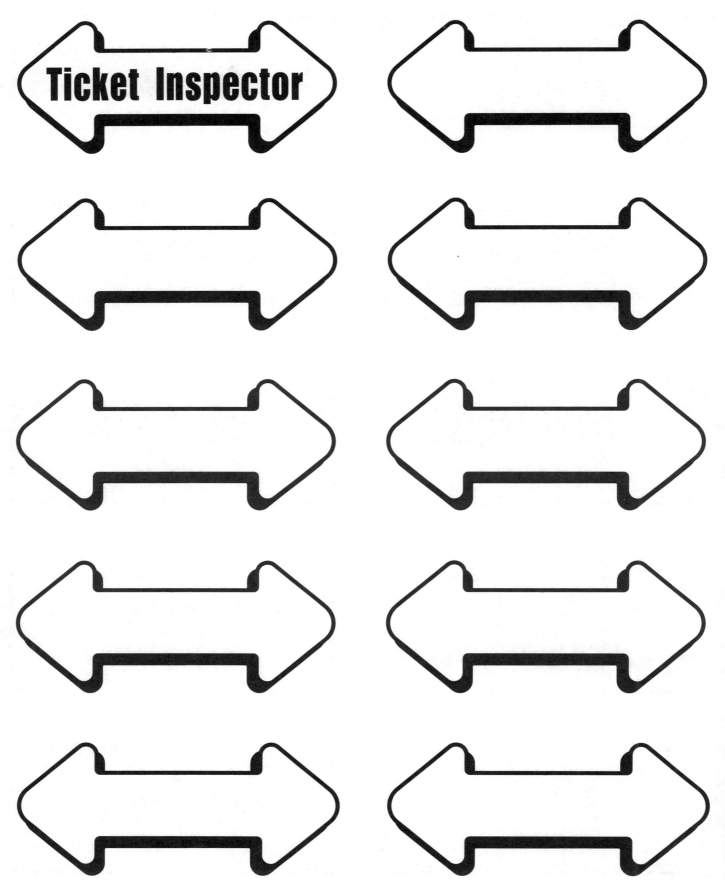

Ticket Inspector

CLASSROOM OF CHOICE

Math log books	Language/Spelling Record
Science log books	Cursive Writing
Learning logs	Writing folders
Math Musings	Math homework books
Everything books	Projects

BLACKLINE MASTERS

Sketchbooks	

Finished math	Finished homework
Finished science	Unfinished work
Other finished work	Work to be filed

CLASSROOM OF CHOICE

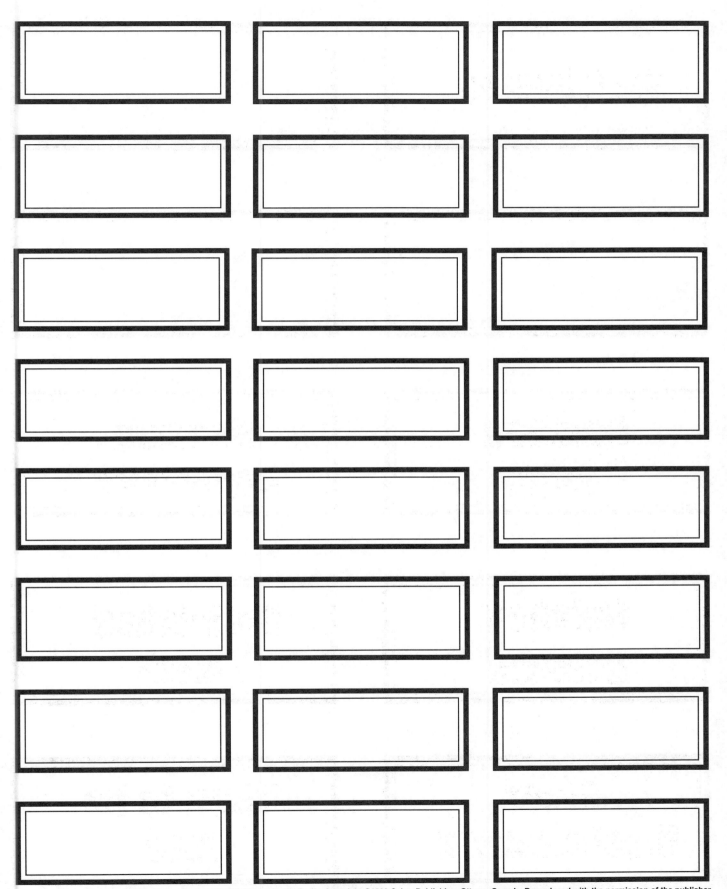

BLACKLINE MASTERS

BLACKLINE MASTERS

CLASSROOM OF CHOICE

Monday	**Saturday**
Tuesday	**Sunday**
Wednesday	**Birthdays**
Thursday	**Newsletter**
Friday	**Days**

Groups

Centres

Year

We have had

School Days

Today is ...

1 Week

Catch-up Day

Free Choice

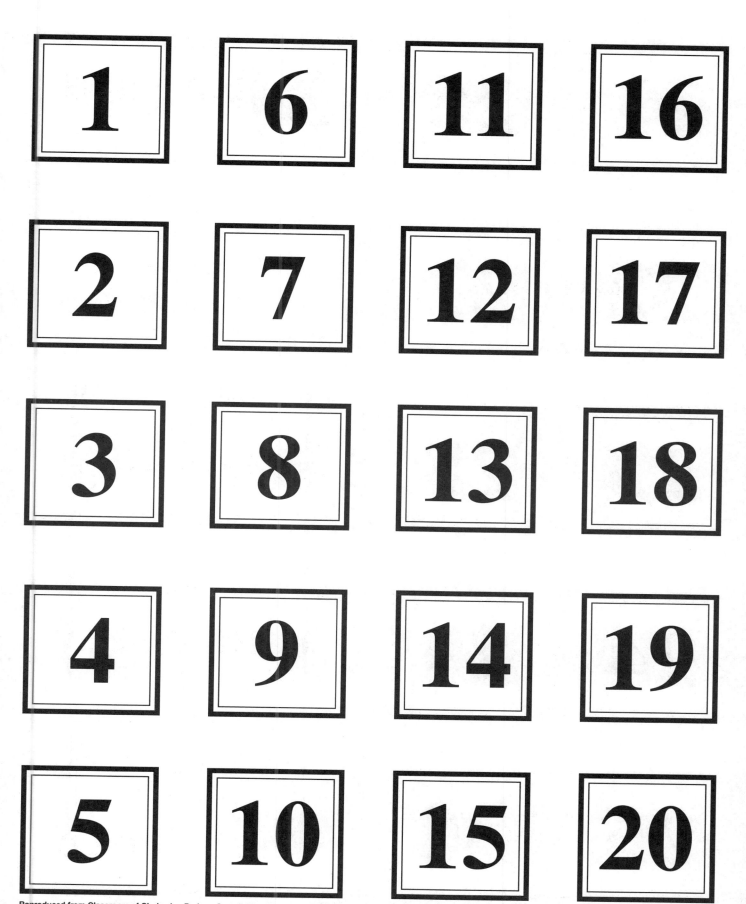

BLACKLINE MASTERS

CLASSROOM OF CHOICE

Total tally for each month:

September has   days.

October has   days.

November has   days.

December has   days.

January has   days.

February has   days.

March has   days.

April has   days.

May has   days.

June has   days.

Yesterday

Tomorrow

Today

CLASSROOM OF CHOICE

MONDAY

TUESDAY

WEDNESDAY

THURSDAY

FRIDAY

SATURDAY

SUNDAY

Monthly tally and number sentence:

CLASSROOM OF CHOICE

JANUARY

FEBRUARY

MARCH

APRIL

MAY

JUNE

JULY

AUGUST

SEPTEMBER

OCTOBER

NOVEMBER

DECEMBER

MY PUBLISHED WORK LIST

NAME:

Finish Date	Type	Title

Type Code: S-story, **R**-research project, **A**-animal research, **C**-country, **P**-poetry, **L**-letter, ☐-poster, **N**-news

CONFERENCE SIGN-UP SHEET

Your name	Date	Type	Title

Type Code: S-story, **R**-research project, **A**-animal research, **C**-country, **P**-poetry, **L**-letter, ☐-poster, **N**-news

CLASS ANIMAL
RESEARCH UPDATE

Your name	Name of Animal	Finish Date

CLASS PUBLISHED WORKS UPDATE

Author	Title of Story	Finish Date

CLASS RESEARCH PROJECT UPDATE

Your name	Name of Research	Finish Date

BLACKLINE MASTERS

PERSONAL PROFILE

This profile was written for _____'s Portfolio.

My full name is _____ .

I am _____ years old. I was born in _____ , _____ .

My birthday is _____ . I have _____ brothers and _____ sisters.

At school, I like _____ , _____ and

_____ . In my free time I like _____

_____ .

I am good at _____ ,

but not so good at _____ .

I wish _____ .

My goal in school is to _____

_____ .

In this picture _____

_____

Date _____

SETTING PERSONAL GOALS

NAME:

DATE:

TERM #:

LONG TERM GOALS

By the end of the year I ...

MEDIUM TERM GOALS

By the end of this term I ...

SHORT TERM GOALS

By the end of this week/month I ...

STEPS TO REACH MY GOALS

... at school	... at home

LOOKING BACK ON THE TERM

NAME:

DATE:

TERM #:

What I learned this term ...

What I have done really well ...

I still need help with ...

I am really proud of ...

Two goals that I would like to reach by next term are ...

I will reach those goals by ...

READER'S RESPONSE TO STUDENT PUBLISHED WORKS

Title:

Writer:

Main theme of the work ...

The work made me feel ...
because ...

I would add ...
because ...

I would change ...

The thing that was written the best was ...

BLACKLINE MASTERS

ART CRITIQUE USING THE SENSES

Look at one painting done by a classmate. Using your senses, describe the painting in as much detail as possible. Talk about the colours, shapes, textures, lines, and depth you see in the artwork. Once you've written your impression of the painting, we will try to guess which painting you are referring to.

Art Critic:

Date:

A thumbnail sketch

I see ...

I feel ...

I think ...

I imagine ...

Work Log

Name _____

Period beginning _____ Period ending _____

Day	Centre Name	Activity Name	Performance	Score	Finished?	Checked
Mon.						
Tues.						
Wed.						
Thurs.						
Fri.						
Mon.						
Tues.						
Wed.						
Thurs.						
Fri.						
Mon.						
Tues.						
Wed.						
Thurs.						
Fri.						
Mon.						
Tues.						
Wed.						
Thurs.						
Fri.						

Level of performance: 1 to 5   Signed off by:

The criteria for assessing your
Level of Performance

After you have completed your job, ask yourself:

1. Did you remain on task for the whole time?

2. Did you use all resources available to you?

3. Did you organize yourself and your materials?

4. Did you review your work for corrections and additions (remember date, centre, and title).

5. Does your work look polished?
(neat writing and coloured drawings)

If you answered yes to :

                1 or 2 questions — fair
                3 or 4 questions — good
                all 5 questions   — Super!

                Give yourself a score out of 5.

PORTFOLIO PRIDE

This selection was made for _____'s Portfolio.   Date _____

I included this work in my portfolio because _____

_____

_____

I did it when _____

_____

I learned _____

_____

PORTFOLIO PRIDE

This selection was made for _____'s Portfolio.   Date _____

This is a sample of my most polished writing because _____

_____

_____

I did it when _____

_____

I learned _____

_____

PORTFOLIO PRIDE

This selection was made for _____'s Portfolio.   Date _____

This is my best science work sample because _____

_____

_____

I did it when _____

_____

I learned _____

_____

PORTFOLIO PRIDE

This selection was made for _____'s Portfolio.   Date _____

I am very proud of this work because _____

_____

_____

I did it when _____

_____

I learned _____

_____

PORTFOLIO PRIDE

This selection was made for _____'s Portfolio.   Date _____

This is what I learned the best in math _____

_____

_____

I did it when _____

_____

I learned _____

_____

PORTFOLIO PRIDE

This selection was made for _____'s Portfolio.   Date _____

I think this is some of my most professional drawing because _____

_____

_____

I did it when _____

_____

I learned _____

_____

PRESENTATION PROPOSAL

To _____ Date _____

I/We would like to do a presentation of the following _____

_____

It would take approximately _____ minutes.

Could you please suggest an appropriate date and time?

Presentation date _____ Presentation time _____

Presenters _____

Sign for approval _____

PERFORMANCE PROPOSAL

To _____ Date _____

I/We would like to do a performance consisting of _____

_____

It would take approximately _____ minutes.

Could you please suggest an appropriate date and time?

Performance date _____ Performance time _____

Performers _____

Sign for approval _____

REVIEW

REVIEW

REVIEW
cont'd

THE NEWS

volume

☐

This month's reporters are:

News reported for the month of:

Our favourite centre was:	Best thing we learned this month:

Students' News

This Month's Hot Topics of Discussion

Teachers' News

Hot! Hot! Hot!

THE NEWS cont'd

Favourite thought of the month:

Favourite book of the month:

Favourite new word:

Favourite joke of the month:

Favourite poem of the month:

School Wide News

Important Reminders

Upcoming Challenges or Events

Good News!

_____

_____

_____

_____

_____

Date _____   From _____

Good News!

_____

_____

_____

_____

_____

Date _____   From _____

Good News!

_____

_____

_____

_____

_____

_____

Date _____ From _____

Good News!

_____

_____

_____

_____

_____

Date _____ From _____

Story Writing Centre

Writer: _____

Title: _____

Date: _____

Editing Checklist

Content

- ☐ The title relates to the story.
- ☐ The introduction grabs the reader's interest.
- ☐ The conclusion makes the story complete.
- ☐ The story makes sense.
- ☐ Nothing is missing from the story.
- ☐ The story is interesting to read.

Mechanics

The following have been checked and corrected:
- ☐ Spelling
- ☐ Capital letters
- ☐ Punctuation
- ☐ Paragraphing

Writer's Responsibility

- ☐ The writer has read this story to me.
- ☐ The writer proofread own work first, & made corrections & changes.

Editor: _____

Story Writing Centre

Writer: _____

Title: _____

Date: _____

Writing Process Checklist

Writing

- ☐ Your plan / web / brainstorming is complete.
- ☐ 1st rough draft is complete.
- ☐ You have read it to two editors.
- ☐ They have completed an editing checklist.
- ☐ You have revised your draft by making changes.
- ☐ You have conferenced with a teacher and made more changes.

Publishing

- ☐ You have typed it on the computer or chosen another form of publication.
- ☐ You have conferenced with a teacher again.
- ☐ You have printed out your good copy.
- ☐ You have glued your book pages.
- ☐ They have been photocopied.
- ☐ You have completed the cover and illustrations.

Date finished: _____

Library Research Request

To: **Our School Librarian**

From: _____

Date: _____

Time: _____

I would like to get some information on:

_____

_____

_____

for my:

_____

_____

_____
Teacher's authorization

Library Research Request

To: **Our School Librarian**

From: _____

Date: _____

Time: _____

I would like to get some information on:

_____

_____

_____

for my:

_____

_____

_____
Teacher's authorization

 **Book Borrowing**

I borrowed this book from the
class Book/Resource Centre:

Title: _____

_____

Author: _____

Borrower: _____

Date: _____

 **Book Borrowing**

I borrowed this book from the
class Book/Resource Centre:

Title: _____

_____

Author: _____

Borrower: _____

Date: _____

 **Book Borrowing**

I borrowed this book from the
class Book/Resource Centre:

Title: _____

_____

Author: _____

Borrower: _____

Date: _____

 **Book Borrowing**

I borrowed this book from the
class Book/Resource Centre:

Title: _____

_____

Author: _____

Borrower: _____

Date: _____

The
Tidy Inspector
is proud of

_____

The
Tidy Inspector
is proud of

_____

_____

You are a
Champion Classroom Cleaner!
You help clean up your group
table and anything else in the
classroom that needs tidying up.

From your friendly
Tidy Inspector

_____

You are a
Champion Classroom Cleaner!
You help clean up your group
table and anything else in the
classroom that needs tidying up.

From your friendly
Tidy Inspector

BLACKLINE MASTERS

Student Supply Request

Date:

Memo from:

The following circled items are needed so I can do my school work.

pencils -6   glue sticks -2

white eraser   box of crayons

set of pencil crayons   work kit box

blue pens -2   postage stamp - 46 cents

large Ziploc bags - 1 box

medium Ziploc bags - 1 box

Student Supply Request

Date:

Memo from:

The following circled items are needed so I can do my school work.

pencils -6   glue sticks -2

white eraser   box of crayons

set of pencil crayons   work kit box

blue pens -2   postage stamp - 46 cents

large Ziploc bags - 1 box

medium Ziploc bags - 1 box

Dear Parents,

Frequently, children are spending valuable time looking for pencils, or borrowing glue sticks. In order to help solve this problem, children will periodically come home with a "student supply request" for items missing from their work kit. We hope this request can be filled as soon as possible. To eliminate frequent requests, when supplying things like pencils and glue sticks, more than one could be purchased and we would be happy to store the extras in a small bag with the student's name on it. Thank you for your co-operation.

Just a little reminder!

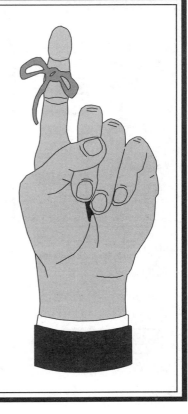

A little reminder for you!

Please Remember!

Book Talk

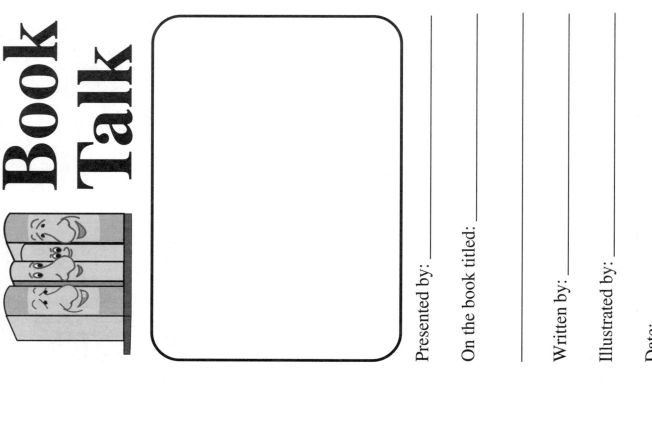

Presented by: _____

On the book titled: _____

Written by: _____

Illustrated by: _____

Date: _____

I/we would recommend this book to a friend because _____
_____
_____
_____

☆☆☆☆☆☆☆☆☆☆

I/we would award this book ____ stars because _____
_____
_____
_____

© 1999 Ottawa, Canada

CEBRA PUBLISHING

This is my/our favourite illustration
in the book. It is _____

_____

_____

_____

I/we picked this book because _____

_____

_____

_____

_____

This book is about _____

_____

_____

It was published in 19 ____

The main character is _____

BLACKLINE MASTERS

Congratulations!

_____

has successfully created

a

Classroom of Choice

by

following the steps in the dynamic teaching model. This will be the beginning of a challenging and rewarding teaching experience which will last a lifetime!

To order a copy of **Classroom of Choice** *for yourself, your school, colleagues or friends*
fill out the mail order form and send it along with your payment to **Cebra Publishing,**
P.O. Box 41063, Elmvale R.P.O. 1910 St. Laurent Blvd., Ottawa, Ontario, Canada K1G 5K9
or fax it to us with payment to follow at (613) 248-3611.

We offer discounts for orders of more than 10 books. Please call us for more details.
In Ottawa (613) 248-3600 Toll free 1-877-49Cebra(1-877-492-3272) **email: cebra@anadas.com**

Don't delay. The number of copies are limited. By ordering now your price of $34.95 is guaranteed.

Mail Order Form

Please send me _____ copies of **Classroom of Choice**

@ 34.95 each   _____

Postage and handling: 1 book/$3.50
2-4 additional books/each $2.00
5 or more books add 5% of total   _____

SUBTOTAL   _____

Canadian residents add 7% G.S.T.   _____

TOTAL AMOUNT ENCLOSED   _____

Enclosed is my   ❑ cheque   ❑ money order   ❑ Mastercard #

| | | | | | | | | | | | | | | | | | | | | | | | |

Name _____

Address _____

City _____   Province _____

Postal code _____   Phone _____

Make all cheques or money orders payable to Cebra Publishing.
Cebra Publishing, P.O. Box 41063, Elmvale R.P.O. 1910 St. Laurent Blvd.,Ottawa, Ontario,
Canada K1G 5K9 (613) 248-3600 Toll Free: 1-877-49Cebra Fax: (613) 248-3611